Suffrage and Women's Writing

This volume examines different types of women's creative writing in support of the demand for the parliamentary vote, including autobiographies, memoirs, letters, diaries, novels, and drama.

The women's suffrage movement became far more visible in the Edwardian period. Large demonstrations and militant actions such as destruction of property were widely reported in the press and reached a wide audience. Eager to get their message across, suffrage campaigners not only took collective action but also used women's creative talents—whether as artists, musicians, or writers—to win hearts and minds for the cause. Through a close reading of contemporary texts, the chapters in this book reveal the diverse nature of the suffrage movement and its ideas, and the complex relationship between the personal and the political. The contributors also highlight the significance of women's writing as a means to advance the suffrage cause and as a key element of suffrage propaganda.

This book was originally published as a special issue of *Women's Writing.*

June Hannam is a Co-chair of the West of England and South Wales Women's History Network and a Professor (emerita) of History at the University of the West of England, Bristol, UK. She edited the *International Encyclopaedia of Women's Suffrage* (with Mitzi Auchterlonie and Katherine Holden, 2000). Her other publications include *Socialist Women: Britain, 1880s to 1920s* (with Karen Hunt, 2001) and *Feminism* (2007).

Katherine Holden is a Co-chair of the West of England and South Wales Women's History Network and was previously a Senior Lecturer at the University of the West of England, Bristol, UK. She edited the *International Encyclopaedia of Women's Suffrage* (with June Hannam and Mitzi Auchterlonie, 2000). Her other publications include *The Shadow of Marriage: Singleness in England, 1914–1960* (2007) and *Nanny Knows Best: The History of the British Nanny* (2013).

Historical Women's Writing

Series editor: Marie Mulvey-Roberts, Professor of English Literature at the University of the West of England, Bristol, UK

This series explores a wide range of women's writing from across the world, spanning several centuries up to the First World War. Each volume consists of a collection of essays focusing on a specific theme, time-period, genre, or author, ranging from the canonical to lesser-known and neglected writers. These books will be a valuable resource for scholars and students of literature and history, as well as for more general readers with an interest in historical women writers and their work.

Recent titles in the series include:

Women's Writing of the First World War
Edited by Emma Liggins and Elizabeth Nolan

Mary Hays's 'Female Biography'
Collective Biography as Enlightenment Feminism
Edited by Mary Spongberg and Gina Luria Walker

Suffrage and Women's Writing
Edited by June Hannam and Katherine Holden

Women's Writing from Wales before 1914
Edited by Jane Aaron

Children's Literature in the Long 19th Century
Edited by Catherine Butler and Ann Alston

Bicentennial Essays on Jane Austen's Afterlives
Edited by Annika Bautz and Sarah Wootton

Locating Ann Radcliffe
Edited by Andrew Smith and Mark Bennett

For a full list of titles please visit https://www.routledge.com/Historical-Womens-Writing/book-series/HWW

Suffrage and Women's Writing

Edited by
June Hannam and Katherine Holden

Routledge
Taylor & Francis Group
LONDON AND NEW YORK

First published 2020
by Routledge
2 Park Square, Milton Park, Abingdon, Oxon, OX14 4RN

and by Routledge
52 Vanderbilt Avenue, New York, NY 10017

Routledge is an imprint of the Taylor & Francis Group, an informa business

British Library Cataloguing-in-Publication Data
A catalogue record for this book is available from the British Library

ISBN13: 978-0-367-35405-3

Typeset in Minion Pro
by codeMantra

Publisher's Note
The publisher accepts responsibility for any inconsistencies that may have arisen during the conversion of this book from journal articles to book chapters, namely the inclusion of journal terminology.

Disclaimer
Every effort has been made to contact copyright holders for their permission to reprint material in this book. The publishers would be grateful to hear from any copyright holder who is not here acknowledged and will undertake to rectify any errors or omissions in future editions of this book.

Contents

Citation Information

The chapters in this book were originally published in *Women's Writing*, volume 25, issue 3 (August 2018). When citing this material, please use the original page numbering for each article, as follows:

Introduction
June Hannam and Katherine Holden
Women's Writing, volume 25, issue 3 (August 2018) pp. 289–293

Chapter 1
"My Part in a Changing World": Women's Struggle for the Vote and the Autobiographical Subject
Mary Joannou
Women's Writing, volume 25, issue 3 (August 2018) pp. 294–313

Chapter 2
"Women Who Dared to Ask for a Vote": The Missing Memoirs of the Scottish Suffragettes
Gemma Elliott
Women's Writing, volume 25, issue 3 (August 2018) pp. 314–328

Chapter 3
Writing Suffrage in Edwardian Nottingham
Val Wood
Women's Writing, volume 25, issue 3 (August 2018) pp. 329–346

Chapter 4
The "Sordid Story" of an Unwanted Child: Militancy, Motherhood and Abortion in Elizabeth Robins' Votes for Women! *and* Way Stations
Emma Liggins
Women's Writing, volume 25, issue 3 (August 2018) pp. 347–361

Chapter 5

The Use of Irony as a Subversive Element in Suffrage Theatre
Veronica Pacheco Costa
Women's Writing, volume 25, issue 3 (August 2018) pp. 362–378

Chapter 6

The American Suffrage Movement and the Novels of Marietta Holley and Elia Peattie as a Means of Cultural Lobbying
Emine Geçgil
Women's Writing, volume 25, issue 3 (August 2018) pp. 379–400

Notes on Contributors

Gemma Elliott is a Postdoctoral Teaching Assistant in English Literature at the University of Glasgow, UK.

Emine Geçgil teaches in the Department of American Culture and Literature and the School of English Language at Bilkent University, Ankara, Turkey. She is a member of the Executive Board of the American Studies Association of Turkey.

June Hannam is a Co-chair of the West of England and South Wales Women's History Network and a Professor (emerita) of History at the University of the West of England, Bristol, UK.

Katherine Holden is a Co-chair of the West of England and South Wales Women's History Network and was previously a Senior Lecturer at the University of the West of England, Bristol, UK.

Mary Joannou is Emerita Professor of Literary History and Women's Writing at Anglia Ruskin University, Cambridge, UK.

Emma Liggins is a Senior Lecturer in English Literature in the Department of English at Manchester Metropolitan University, UK.

Veronica Pacheco Costa is a Senior Lecturer at Pablo de Olavide University, Seville, Spain.

Val Wood is an Independent Researcher and Social Historian based in Nottingham, UK. In 2009, she co-founded the Nottingham Women's History Group.

Introduction

June Hannam and Katherine Holden

In this year of commemorating the passing of the 1918 Representation of the People Act that enfranchised some women over the age of 30, the emphasis has been on women's campaigning for the vote and the methods and tactics they employed to achieve it. During the Edwardian period, all the suffrage organizations became far more visible: they held large demonstrations, sold their newspapers on the street and raised money for the cause.[1] Militants from the Women's Social and Political Union destroyed property, went to prison, and suffered hunger strikes and forcible feeding, while the National Union of Women's Suffrage Societies organized the impressive 1913 Pilgrimage, when women walked from all corners of Britain to meet up at a large rally in London.[2] One aim of these activities was to win hearts and minds, and to put as much pressure as possible on politicians and the government. An integral part of such campaigning was the use of women's creative talents, whether as artists, musicians or writers. Lisa Tickner has argued persuasively that posters and banners were not just a colourful footnote to, but an integral part of, the struggle for the vote, and helped to create an image of what it meant to be a political woman in the twentieth century.[3] Increasing attention has also been paid to the significance of women's writing as a means of advancing the cause of suffrage and as yet another method of achieving social change. This special issue of *Women's Writing* seeks to add to our understanding of the power of creative writing both to shape contemporary ideas and to influence the later interpretations of historians. At the same time, through detailed investigations of suffrage life writing, drama and fiction, it points to ways in which a close reading of contemporary texts can reveal the diverse nature of the suffrage movement and its ideas, and encourage us to explore the complex interrelationship between the personal and the political.

Many suffragists and suffragettes wrote memoirs and autobiographies which highlighted their years in the suffrage movement.[4] For some, the suffrage campaign was just part of a longer story of political activism, whereas for others it was the main event. The autobiographies of leading militant campaigners have received most attention. It has been suggested that they have created a view of the authentic militant as someone who went to prison and suffered forcible feeding, and that this has had a long-standing influence on the interpretations of historians.[5] Three of the articles in this special issue examine autobiographical writings across a broader spectrum. Maroula Joannou looks at 20 autobiographies from different parts of the movement and claims that this provides a variegated, complex and diverse picture of "the cause, its fault line and its supporters". At the same time, there are many similarities. For all of them, the suffrage struggle was the "crucible" in which their political understanding was shaped, and they all looked back on their experience of the vote as life-changing. Joannou includes those who are often excluded from a narrative that focuses on the "authentic militant", but also acknowledges that militancy was significant for overturning old ways of thinking about what it meant to be a woman. She concludes that an autobiography is a political act because it asserts a right to speak rather than to be spoken for.

Gemma Elliott, on the other hand, provides a more detailed account of two suffragette autobiographies, by Elizabeth Thomson and Jessie Stephen, who were members of the Scottish Women's Social and Political Union. These do not figure so often in discussions of suffragette autobiography since, as unpublished manuscripts housed respectively in the University of Glasgow and the Manchester Working-Class Movement Library, they are less accessible to both researchers and general readers. And yet they provide new information on the diversity of the movement. As Elliott suggests, Elizabeth Thomson, from a family of doctors and academics, was unusual in first becoming involved in suffrage campaigning in her sixties, in 1909, and then taking part in militant actions which led to her imprisonment. The interest of Jessie Stephen, on the other hand, is that she was a working-class trade union activist who joined the militant suffrage movement and later linked suffrage and socialist politics. The autobiographies provide an interesting contrast in style, tone and content. Thomson wrote her autobiography just before the 1918 Act was passed, and her story is intertwined with that of her sister, who was also involved in militancy. Stephen's manuscript was written towards the end of her life and covers the many different facets of a long career in politics. Thomson provides information on dates and events, whereas Stephen's account is more concerned with emotions and anecdotes about the women she worked with. In focusing on two suffrage campaigners from Scotland, Elliott also draws our attention to the need to move away from London in order to gain a wider perspective on the nature of the suffrage movement.

This is also the intention of Val Wood's article, which explores the writings of three women, from different parts of the movement, who were engaged in suffrage campaigning in Nottingham: the suffragist Helena Dowson and the suffragettes Nellie Crocker and Helen Watts. Their writings took different forms. Helena Dowson wrote diaries, which then formed part of a biography written about her by her granddaughter, Alix Meynell; Nellie Crocker produced an unpublished autobiography, deposited at Girton College, Cambridge; and Helen Watts wrote out her speeches, which were then deposited in the Nottinghamshire Archives. Such varied pieces of writing add different perspectives, but what they all show is the extensive nature of the suffrage campaign in Nottingham, the ways in which the lives of all three women were intertwined, and the sympathy shown to the militants by Dowson in the face of local public criticism of all the groups.

In her article, Emma Liggins also examines varied forms of writing as a way to highlight the diversity of the suffrage movement. In this case, they are all the writings of one woman: the former actress Elizabeth Robins.[6] *Way Stations* is a collection of speeches, articles and letters to the press with an innovative structure that intersperses the description of key events with autobiographical fragments. Robins uses this form to analyse the merits of militancy compared with the more "quiet form" of rebellion of the ordinary woman. Liggins concludes that *Way Stations* is less a defence of militancy and more a recognition of the diverse ways in which women could participate in the cause. At the same time, Robins used her play *Votes for Women* as a space where she could explore the different ways in which women could live their lives beyond the usual roles of wives and sweethearts. She touched on the controversial questions of contraception and abortion, and on childlessness as a positive choice that could be made by women, thereby using her fictional writing to create the possibility of choice and of personal as well as social change.

Katharine Cockin and Naomi Paxton have written extensively on the significant contribution of suffrage plays and playwrights to the propaganda of the suffrage movement.[7] In her article in this special issue, Veronica Pacheco Costa takes a detailed look at the use of irony in plays by different authors. She suggests that they were "funny, mocking and entertaining" as they provided a critique of women's social position. In some cases, they dealt with actual events, such as episodes that occurred on a picket line outside the House of Commons in 1909, which was the subject of Alice Chapin's play *At the Gates*, or with problems and inequalities faced by women in the workplace. Other plays made a comedy out of social norms, such as Cicely Hamilton and Christopher St John's play *How the Vote Was Won*, which depicted the difficulties faced by Horace when all his female relatives left their jobs and turned up asking for his support. In all these cases, Pacheco Costa concludes that comic irony was used to convince audiences that women had legitimate grievances, and thereby turned irony into "a subversive tool".

Novels provided a further space in which to explore new ways of thinking and different ways of living for women.[8] Emine Gecgil's article examines two novelists from the American suffrage movement: Elia Wilkinson Peattie and Marietta Holley. They both sought to encourage women to take up the cause of women's suffrage and, in particular, to counter the arguments of anti-suffragists, but they targeted different audiences and therefore the tone and content are also different. Marietta Holley aimed her novel *Samantha on the Woman Question* at an older, rural audience, and uses homely wisdom and dialect, laced with humour, which would appear less threatening. Elia Wilkinson Peattie, on the other hand, based her novel *The Precipice* on the life of a young social reformer, who tries to balance her career with competing family demands, and she targeted her fiction at the "modern" urban woman at work. In both cases, however, Gecgil argues that the novels advocated suffrage as a means to achieve social change, but aimed to be more effective in their propaganda by not undermining the socially acceptable gender norms of their white middle-class audience.

It has long been recognized that involvement in the struggle for the suffrage changed women's view of themselves and what they were capable of, as well as achieving the goal of enfranchisement. One way in which their aspirations were expressed was through the use of art, literature and other forms of women's writing. Suffrage campaigners were convinced that "artists and intellectuals had a key role to play in bringing about cultural change".[9] The articles in this special issue have sought to highlight the importance of different types of women's suffrage writing both for the suffrage campaign and for women themselves, and in doing so they contribute to our appreciation of the richness and diversity of the suffrage movement.

Notes

1. Harold L. Smith, *The British Women's Suffrage Campaign, 1866–1928*, 2nd ed. (Harlow: Pearson Education, 2007); Elizabeth Crawford, *The Women's Suffrage Movement: A Reference Guide, 1866–1928* (London: Routledge, 1999).
2. Krista Cowman, *Women of the Right Spirit: Paid Organisers of the Women's Social and Political Union (WSPU) 1904–18* (Manchester: Manchester UP, 2007); Jane Robinson, *Hearts and Minds: The Untold Story of the Great Pilgrimage and How Women Won the Vote* (London: Doubleday, 2018).
3. Lisa Tickner, *The Spectacle of Women: Imagery of the Suffrage Campaign 1907–14* (London: Chatto, 1987).
4. Maroula Joannou, "She Who Would Be Politically Free Herself Must Strike the First Blow: Suffragette Autobiography and Suffragette Militancy", *The Uses of Autobiography*, ed. Julia Swindells (London: Taylor and Francis, 1995), pp. 31–44.
5. Hilda Kean, "Searching for the Present in Past Defeat: The Construction of Historical and Political Identity in British Feminism in the 1920s and 1930s", *Women's History Review*, 3.1 (1994): 57–80; Laura E. Nym Mayhall, "Creating the Suffragette Spirit: British Feminism and the Historical Imagination", *Women's History Review*, 4.3 (1995): 319–44.

6. Angela V. John, *Elizabeth Robins: Staging a Life* (London: History, 2007).
7. Katharine Cockin, *Women and Theatre in the Age of Suffrage: The Pioneer Players, 1911–1925* (Basingstoke: Palgrave, 2000); Naomi Paxton, "Very Much Alive and Kicking: The Actresses' Franchise League from 1914–1928", *Stage Women: Female Theatre Workers, Professional Practice and Agency in the Early Twentieth Century*, ed. Maggie B. Gale and Kate Dorney (Manchester: Manchester UP, 2017).
8. Maroula Joannou, "Suffragette Fiction and the Fictions of Suffrage", *The Women's Suffrage Movement: New Feminist Perspectives*, ed. June Purvis and Maroula Joannou (Manchester: Manchester UP, 1998), pp. 101–16.
9. Maroula Joannou and June Purvis, "Introduction: The Writing of the Women's Suffrage Movement", Purvis and Joannou, p. (11).

Disclosure statement

No potential conflict of interest was reported by the authors.

"MY PART IN A CHANGING WORLD": WOMEN'S STRUGGLE FOR THE VOTE AND THE AUTOBIOGRAPHICAL SUBJECT

Mary Joannou

ABSTRACT

This essay is concerned with some 20 autobiographies by participants in the women's suffrage movement with differing backgrounds and beliefs. Their writings reveal similarities and differences between autobiographical subjects. The author addresses the importance that some autobiographers attached to pain, the problems attendant on its representation, and their determination to make women's pain count politically. The autobiographical accounts of Helena Swanwick, Millicent Garrett Fawcett, Edith Picton-Turbevill and other suffragists are contrasted to the suffragette autobiographies of Emmeline Pankhurst and her supporters, with their emphasis on law-breaking, imprisonment and patriotic support for the war effort. The struggle for the vote was the apogee of some women's lives, while for others a mere stepping stone; their life achievements lay elsewhere—in the peace movement, the theatre, social reform, music, religion, the police service or journalism. However, the autobiographical subjects look back on the excitement of the suffrage struggles as life-changing—the crucible in which their subsequent political understanding was shaped. In paying critical attention to the writings of militant and non-militant, Christian and secularist, socialist and fascist alike, the author shows how these autobiographies create a variegated, complex and diverse picture of the "cause", its fault lines and its supporters.

This essay is concerned with some 20 autobiographies written by participants in the women's suffrage movement.[1] I examine the autobiographical writing of women of differing social backgrounds and political persuasions in relation to some feminist theoretical accounts of autobiography which help to illuminate both the usefulness of the genre to supporters of the movement and why this has been a genre of writing historically important to women. I also explore some of the objectives and priorities of different activists, the tensions which arose from them in the Edwardian and post-Edwardian suffrage movement, and how those tensions inform their later autobiographies.

As is customary, I use the word "suffragist" to describe supporters of the National Union of Women's Suffrage Societies (NUWSS), founded in 1897, and others who worked for the vote by constitutional means. The word "suffragette" is used to denote supporters of the Women's Social and Political Union (WSPU), started in 1903, the Women's Freedom League, formed in 1907, and others who resorted to militant action.[2] However, many varieties of suffragism were to be found across the country. Women altered their loyalties and started and joined new local and regional groups. Some organizations were set up nationally to bring together those with shared professional, occupational, political or religious interests. This was the case for the Women Writers' Suffrage League, of which one of my autobiographical subjects, Cicely Hamilton, was a member, and the Church League for Women's Suffrage, to which another, Margaret Wynne Nevinson, belonged.

While the rights of men to tell their own life stories have historically been uncontentious, women's attempts to do likewise have been fraught with difficulty. Concluding her memoir, published alongside her biography of her deceased husband in 1656, Margaret Cavendish, Duchess of Newcastle asks: "Why hath this lady writ her own life?" Anticipating a question that could have been addressed to anyone having the temerity to write her own autobiography in a society in which the personal life of a woman was regarded as being of lesser consequence than that of a man, she responds thus:

> [...] tis no purpose to the readers, but it is to the authoress because I write for my own sake, not theirs; neither did I intend this piece for to delight, but to divulge; not to please the fancy, but to tell the truth.[3]

By 1935, it appears that little had changed in this respect. The suffragist Helena Swanwick, a pioneering journalist with the *Manchester Guardian* and a British representative at the League of Nations, still felt the need to preface her autobiography with fulsome praise for her late husband and this modest disclaimer of any public significance of her own: "To write, nay more, to offer for publication, a whole book strung on the thread of one's own personality seems an outburst of egotism requiring apology".[4] An alternative reading of Swanwick's words, however, is that they are an attempt to dissociate herself from the romantic heroism of the autobiographies of some militant suffragettes which celebrate the "willful acts of heroic individuals bent on making themselves forces of change".[5]

Propelled from obscurity to the limelight by the struggle with which their names are inextricably linked, Millicent Garrett Fawcett and Christabel, Emmeline and Sylvia Pankhurst were, and indeed still are, well known; Helena Swanwick was somewhat less so. All their autobiographies fulfil the "classic" criterion of what constitutes a good autobiography: that this should demonstrate and illuminate the subject's links to the times in which they live. Yet the conflation of male subjectivity and human identity remained so strong that Margaret Cavendish's question ("Why hath this lady writ her own life?") resonates across autobiographies published several centuries later. As Sidonie Smith puts it: "From their position of marginality, women have spoken. They have written public autobiography. Nonetheless, when they engage in the autobiographical project, they did so as interlopers".[6]

These autobiographical writings about suffrage are remarkable in their range and diversity, and cannot without the grossest distortion be assimilated to any common grid. They indicate similarities between women as well as significant differences. I return later to some of these key differences: the importance that some autobiographies (but not others) attached to pain, the problems attendant on its representation, and the determination of some autobiographers to make women's pain count politically. There are also differences of emphasis on continuity with the nineteenth-century struggles and on change, as in the WSPU's innovative and disruptive strategy and tactics. Participation in the struggle was the apogee of some women's lives, while for others it was merely a stepping stone; their major life achievements lay elsewhere or were still to come in, for example, the peace movement, the theatre, social reform, music, religion, the police service or journalism. However, virtually without exception, the autobiographical subjects look back on the excitement of having worked for the vote as life-changing and acknowledge themselves as beneficiaries of, as well as participants in, the struggle.

Their writings pay tribute to the suffrage struggle as the crucible in which their political understanding was shaped. "The education I received as a political agitator was enhanced a hundredfold by the fact that I received it from Dame Millicent Garrett Fawcett, my leader", wrote the preacher Maude Royden, who edited the NUWSS journal the *Common Cause.*[7] Royden obtained her "suffrage education" working with the poor at the Victoria Women's Settlement in Liverpool, and is remembered today for her pioneering work for the ordination of women in the Church of England.

As I have argued elsewhere, suffragette autobiography is largely a misnomer insofar as militancy lasted some 10 years, was suspended in 1914 and could hardly constitute the *raison d'être* of any woman's entire adult life.[8] The suffragette narrative, in which the emotional and physical trauma of imprisonment and forcible feeding is related by women who lived through these ordeals (including Lady Constance Lytton, Emily Wilding Davison, and Christabel and Emmeline Pankhurst), is deeply embedded in the public consciousness. Indeed, it is widely recognized as representing the ultimate in women's commitment, courage, idealism and capacity for personal sacrifice for a higher cause.[9]

Yet, as Laura Mayhall has shown, what can be loosely termed the "suffragette trauma narrative" is largely a retrospective construction consolidated during the 1920s and 1930s, and owing much to the activities of the former suffragettes who set up the Suffragette Fellowship for the purpose of memorializing the bravery of the militants and ensuring that their version of the historical record should never be forgotten.[10] This is, however, but one of a number of competing and contested narratives relating to women's struggle for the vote available to women at the time and to historians in later years. The autobiographical accounts of the public dimensions of the suffrage movement and its impact on the personal lives of women such as Helena Swanwick, Millicent Garrett Fawcett and Edith Picton-Turbevill, who did not believe it right to break the law and had no first-hand experiences of prison, position them outside the dominant narrative of women's enfranchisement. This is associated primarily with Emmeline and Christabel Pankhurst and their emphasis on the need for militancy, law-breaking, imprisonment and patriotic support for the war effort between 1914 and 1918. It is by looking at these autobiographies collectively, paying attention to the words of militant and non-militant, avid Christian and secularist, socialist and fascist alike, that I hope to show how they can help us to form a more variegated, complex and diverse picture of the "cause", its fault lines and its supporters than has hitherto been recognized.

As Leigh Gilmore suggests, the authority of autobiography "is derived through autobiography's proximity to the rhetoric of truth telling: the confession",[11] judicial and spiritual—that is, the autobiographical subject telling a "truth" which can be externally verified, the disclosure of which is important both to her identity and subjectivity and to the textual production of the autobiographical self. Yet autobiographical inscription is by its nature self-justificatory. The memory, as James Olney notes, "goes backward so that narrative, its twin and counterpart, may go forward: memory and narration move along the same line only in reverse directions".[12] Thus, the suffrage autobiographers frequently punctuate their narratives with reflections on criticisms of their actions of which they were unaware at the time of the events they narrate. They do this to justify their past behaviour to future generations with no memory of the world without the hard-won freedoms their actions helped to bring about. Autobiographical writing by women attempts to put straight the historical record, but the disclosure of public facts is inseparable from the private subjectivities of the narratorial "I". Autobiography is a genre in which the self is authorized, but, because the narration of a life can never be restricted to a solitary isolated subject, it is also and always far more than a self-authorizing genre.

The relationship between the individual and organized suffragism was symbiotic: the development of an individual political consciousness predicated on the development of women's collective political consciousness, and vice versa. As Tess Cosslett, Celia Lury and Penny Summerfield put it, the "narration of a self cannot be understood in isolation from another it acknowledges, implicitly or explicitly, and with which it is in a constitutive relationship", and such "others" are "an integral part of consciousness, events and the production of a narrative".[13] The autobiographies show how the shared experience of militant action engendered lifelong personal friendships, sisterhood and solidarity: "You have a different feeling all your life about the women with whom you eluded the police sleuth and went forth to break windows in Whitehall, or to be mobbed in Parliament Square, or ejected from a Cabinet Minister's meeting", noted the journalist Evelyn Sharp.[14] "There is a cord between Christabel and me that nothing can break—the cord of love. Distance or absence makes no difference. We started Militancy side by side and we stood together until Victory was won", wrote Lancashire textile worker Annie Kenney.[15]

The autobiographical subject's sense of identification with a wider community (the women's suffrage movement) and with what Bella Brodski and Celeste Schenck refer to as "singularity in alternity"—the representation of the self in relation to others—is essential to the informed understanding of their personal narratives.[16] Yet the idea of community that permeates the life writings is problematic—exclusionary as well as inclusive. Women chose to shift their allegiances from one community to another, to change the communities they joined, and to alter their relationship to those they left behind.

It is worth pausing to consider some of the fissions and tensions that inform the autobiographies. As Millicent Garrett Fawcett explained:

> [...] the general mass of suffragists throughout the country were loyal to the cause by whomsoever it was represented, just as Italian patriots in the great days of the *Risorgimento* supported the unity of Italy, whether promoted by Cavour, Garibaldi or Mazzini.[17]

However, the autobiographers reveal differences of principle which were deeply held and often irreconcilable. The WSPU was founded in Manchester in 1903 by Emmeline Pankhurst, a member of the Independent Labour Party from 1893–1903, and of the NUWSS. The first major split within the WSPU occurred in 1907 when disaffected members, asking for a constitution, the devolution of powers to local groups and democratic accountability within the organization, voted to form the Women's Freedom League; they carried with them approximately 20% of the WSPU membership.[18] Many of the rebels were socialists who wanted the WSPU to be closer to the labour movement. Prominent members of the League included Charlotte Despard, Margaret Wynne Nevinson, Teresa Billington-Greig, Edith How-Martyn, Dora Marsden, Helena Normanton and Anne Cobden Sanderson.

Emmeline Pethick-Lawrence and her husband Frederick were ousted from the WSPU by Emmeline and Christabel Pankhurst in 1912 when it became clear that men were no longer welcome in the organization and that criticism of extreme militant tactics would not be tolerated. Evelyn Sharp left in solidarity with the Pethick-Lawrences and the three joined the United Suffragists. This group, which was open to men and to non-militants, was started in

1914 in response to the acceleration of suffragette violence and disaffection with the separatist policies of the WSPU leadership. The radical suffragists, in the main Lancashire textile operatives and the East London Federation of Suffragettes led by Sylvia Pankhurst, retained their commitment to socialist politics and fought for the rights of working women and their children, as well as the vote. Finally, the largest of the societies, the NUWSS, was subject to an existential crisis of massive proportions, to which I return, over the question of women's support for the 1914–18 war. This split the society into diametrically opposed pacifist and non-pacifist camps, and led to some important feminist peace initiatives in which Sharp, Helena Swanwick and Emmeline Pethick-Lawrence were prominent.

In practice, "[r]ank-and-file suffragists were often either oblivious of, or indifferent to, the divisions among the national leadership, or between that leadership and the leadership of the labour movement".[19] Many belonged to more than one suffrage organization, including Sylvia Pankhurst, Evelyn Sharp, Margaret Wynne Nevinson, Hannah Mitchell, Maud Arncliffe Sennett, Mary Gawthorpe, Dora Montefiore, Cicely Hamilton, Charlotte Despard and Emmeline Pethick-Lawrence. In *Life Errant* (1935), Cicely Hamilton, who wrote the lyrics of the suffrage anthem "The March of the Women", explains:

> For a few months I was a member of the Women's Social and Political Union; then, for somewhat longer, of the Women's Freedom League; but I was happier working with less political bodies, such as the Women Writers' Suffrage League, of which I was one of the founders.[20]

Dora Montefiore was active in socialist circles and a WSPU executive member. Her autobiography, *From a Victorian to a Modern* (1927), provides a vivid account of the renowned "Siege of Hammersmith" in 1906 when she withheld her taxes and barricaded herself into her house to await the bailiffs, surrounded by fervent supporters. Montefiore became Honorary Secretary of the Adult Suffrage Society at the request of its President, the shopworkers' leader Margaret Bondfield. The move reflected her disenchantment with suffragette violence—"I could not reconcile myself to seeing the young girls resisting, with physical force, the police".[21] It also reflected the strength of her socialist convictions, as the WSPU moved further away from its labour movement origins, and her commitment to the enfranchisement of working men.

The foundation of the WSPU amounted to a shift in the tectonic plates in the history of suffragism in the United Kingdom, dramatically moving the vote to the heart of the political agenda from the peripheries and challenging not only the Liberal government but also the deeply rooted assumptions and ways of working of the constitutionalist suffragists. In order to understand the strength of feeling—the cumulative anger, hope, disappointment and frustration that underpinned suffragette activity—it should be remembered that half a century of lobbying for the vote by an indefatigable band of Victorian and Edwardian constitutional suffragists had proved largely to no avail. Only 2 of the 18 bills that were put before the House (in 1875 and 1886), in the period between John Stuart Mill's amendment to the Reform Bill of 1867 and the start of suffragette militancy, passed a second reading. The rest were all defeated, obstructed or thrown out, in what Margaret Wynne Nevinson aptly summarized in Life's Fitful Fever (1926) as a "wonderful record of women's patience and men's shame".[22]

However, the methods of the NUWSS, led by the veteran Millicent Garrett Fawcett since 1897, were courteous, ladylike and restrained—so much so that Maud Arncliffe Sennett, a West End actor active in the Actresses' Franchise League who performed under the stage name of Mary Kingsley, professed herself to be unaware of its existence in her autobiography, *The Child* (1938): "For it is a dead certainty that though I had been all my life, longing for the upliftment of my sex, I knew nothing of this older society".[23] Indeed, when militancy erupted, Sennett was forcibly struck by the contrast between the two sections:

> The militant women look so much younger, progressive and with so much more *life* in them, though younger they were not. And looking at these groups, I seem to see why Mrs Fawcett's party had been on the road for so many years and almost needed the inspiration of Christabel Pankhurst and her young followers to put life into the movement.[24]

Of course, not all women who wanted to take part in militant actions were in a position to do so. Evelyn Sharp was constrained from breaking the law by a promise from which she was released after five years in 1911 by a letter from her mother. Jane Sharp conceded that: "I have no right to thwart you, much as I should regret feeling that you were undergoing those terrible hardships".[25] The author Violet Hunt would

> [...] certainly have done my three months in the terrible second division if it had not been for the provisions I made for the care, delegated to me, of an invalid mother and a young niece. Mrs Pankhurst and Christabel kindly dispensed with my services *in extremis*.[26]

Annie Barnes "had commitments at home looking after all my brothers and sisters. I couldn't chance imprisonment". But she "did volunteer for other things that were less risky".[27] Her first mission with the East London Federation of Suffragettes was to throw leaflets over London from the top of the Monument.

The suffrage campaigns bifurcated women's lives into a modern "after" and a Victorian and Edwardian "before". Mary Sophia Allen, who became a high ranking woman police officer, recollects the shock of leaving home after her father's ultimatum to "give up this Suffragette nonsense absolutely and for good—or you leave this house!"[28] Other autobiographical subjects railed against domestic and marital ideologies which put obstacles in the way of their creativity, personal fulfilment and intellectual endeavour. Helena Swanwick was at loggerheads with her mother: "I had felt and resented the assumption that, whereas education was of importance for my brothers it was of no account for me", she writes in *I Have Been Young* (1935). She adds:

> A boy might be a person, but not a girl. This was the ineradicable root of our differences. All my brothers had rights as persons; not I. Till I married (at the age of 24) she never, in her heart, conceded me personal rights.[29]

The arguments against marriage that Cicely Hamilton had articulated in her feminist treatise *Marriage as a Trade* (1909) are reiterated in her autobiography. She explains that "what I rebelled at chiefly was the dependence implied in the idea of 'destined' marriage, 'destined' motherhood—the identification of success with marriage, of failure with spinsterhood, the artificial concentration of the hopes of girlhood on sexual attraction and maternity".[30]

The women's suffrage movement was a cultural, social and political network in which feminist ideas were hegemonic, and which provided supporters with education, resources, sisterhood and support. As Liz Stanley explains: "feminism constitutes an ontology, a different way of being in the world which is rooted in the facts of oppression".[31] The movement acted as a magnet for women who had experienced discrimination professionally and in their personal lives, and who were often just as interested in the feminist transformation of society which the vote symbolized as in the vote itself: "My personal revolt was feminist rather than suffragist", writes Hamilton.[32] Maude Royden explained that

> [...] to work for the enfranchisement of women was a tremendous experience, a tremendous education [...] The struggle both absorbed and widened my life. It gave me a sympathy—and I believe an understanding which linked me to all disfranchised persons and nations.[33]

Participation in the campaigns brought action, excitement, lustre and agency to sheltered lives hitherto starved of meaning and purpose. Annie Barnes recalls: "Being in the suffragettes did a lot for me. I couldn't say 'Boo' to a goose before that".[34] Writer after writer values the movement because it validated the intensity of feeling that she had experienced, perhaps for the first time in her life. In *This Was My World* (1933), Margaret, Lady Rhondda wrote:

> [...] for many other young women like me, militant suffrage was the very salt of life. The knowledge of it had come like a draught of fresh air into our padded, stilted lives [...] It made us feel that we were part of life, not just outside watching it. It made us feel that we had a real purpose and use apart from having children.[35]

As Kathryn Dodd suggests, the suffragette autobiographers created a new "public identity" in which the "personal" became "re-defined" and "transformed by public life".[36] Titles such as *This Was My World*, *My Part in a Changing World* (1938) and *From a Victorian to a Modern* linked the individual to the collective and the personal journey described to wider societal changes in the position of women. The autobiographies evoke the repressiveness of women's lives in Edwardian and Victorian Britain, in which restrictive hemlines and chaperones for unmarried women were de rigueur. Lady Rhondda recalls:

> [...] it required an almost unbelievable effort of will before a woman brought up with all the inhibitions of the decent Victorian "lady" could bring herself to throw stones through a street window. The women who did it broke more than windows with their stones; they broke the crust and conventions of a whole era.[37]

Margaret Wynne Nevinson, a clergyman's daughter, had begun her adult life as a "decent Victorian 'Lady'" and struggled to overcome her inhibitions before making her debut as a public speaker outside some gasworks in south London in 1906: "At first I refused to speak at street corners and in the open; I could not overcome my Victorian prejudices; it seemed such a vulgar thing to do".[38] In Life's Fitful Fever Nevinson describes an outdoor meeting at Waterloo as a "nightmare of horror" with a "volley of rotten tomatoes, cabbage stalks and decayed fruit".[39] But indoor meetings were also fraught with dangers. The water hose was turned on at a meeting of the Women's Freedom League at Sutton in 1907, where "wild pandemonium reigned; rats were let loose amongst the audience".[40] Violet Hunt recollects her discomfiture on rattling a collecting tin with May Sinclair, another member of the Women Writers' Suffrage League:

> Much has been said about our heroism in "standing outside to beg", and I fancy she felt as I did—as if we had suddenly been stripped naked, with a cross-sensation of being drowned in a tank and gasping for breath.[41]

Not all autobiographers shared the privileged middle-class upbringings of Nevinson, Hunt and Sinclair. Mary Gawthorpe, Annie Kenney, Hannah Mitchell and Molly Murphy remind us of the origins of the women's suffrage movement in the labour movement, and of its deep working class roots in the north of England. Their autobiographies evoke the richness of a forgotten culture of Sunday schools, churches, choirs, discussion groups, cooperative societies, Clarion cycling clubs and self-help groups set up by socialists and political radicals to bring culture, enlightenment and enjoyment of outdoor activities to working-class lives governed by unrelenting poverty and toil. Molly Murphy (neé Morris), a WSPU organizer in Sheffield, had joined the Manchester WSPU at 16 years of age through her mother, an ardent co-operator and diligent reader of the *Clarion* newspaper. She recollects that the "first two years of the WSPU were spent mainly in propaganda in Labour Party branches, Clarion clubs, trade union branches, open air meetings, during the 'wakes' in the cotton towns".[42]

Gawthorpe, Kenney and Mitchell tell how they were politicized in a flourishing network of socialist choirs, Sunday schools, Clarion clubs, trade union and Independent Labour Party branches, etc., which transported working-class women like themselves out of the home and gave them a political education and new organizational skills. "The Labour Movement, it now seemed to me, was in aim and method all I had hitherto known as practical Christianity. I took to the new ethics like a duck to water", wrote Gawthorpe, a school teacher and Independent Labour Party and National Union of Teachers activist in Leeds, who was appointed as a WSPU organizer in Manchester after she met Christabel Pankhurst, and was a "demure young lady of exactly 24 who spoke at the Sunday night meeting of the Labour Church".[43]

One of 12 children, Annie Kenney had worked full-time in a cotton mill in Oldham from the age of 13 before becoming a WSPU organizer. "The changed life into which most of us entered was a revolution in itself", wrote Kenney in *Memories of a Militant* (1924):

> No home-life, no one to say what we should do or what we should not do, no family ties, we were free and alone in a great brilliant city, scores of young women scarcely out of their teens met together in a revolutionary movement, outlaws or breakers of laws, independent of everything and everybody, fearless and self-confident.[44]

Hannah Mitchell, later to become a magistrate and member of Manchester City Council, was also appointed as a WSPU organizer. Mitchell struggled to support herself as a seamstress while her husband insisted she fulfil the domestic duties he still expected. In consequence, she suffered exhaustion and a minor nervous breakdown, writing in *The Hard Way Up* (1977), published posthumously by her grandson, that "no cause was ever won between dinner and tea, and those of us who were married had to fight with one hand tied behind us".[45]

While some autobiographical subjects were motivated by socialist principles, others recall the deep religious convictions that underpinned their activism. References to conversion, suffering and martyrdom permeated suffrage discourse. Lady Constance Lytton and Emily Wilding Davison were "martyrs", and Saint Joan was the "patron saint" of the movement. Indeed, NUWSS supporters on the Women's Pilgrimage in 1913 followed the traditional routes taken by medieval pilgrims. "For—let there be no mistake about it—this movement was not primarily political; it was social, moral, psychological and profoundly religious", explained Swanwick.[46]

Lesley Parker Hume notes that the members of the executive committee of the NUWSS were generally middle-aged, mostly middle class, and Evangelical or Nonconformist in religion, with a high proportion of Quakers among them.[47] Charlotte Despard, President of the Women's Freedom League, converted to Roman Catholicism out of respect for the religion of the working-class Irish Catholic community in Battersea among whom she lived. Emmeline Pethick-Lawrence describes how her lifelong commitment to the poor began as a voluntary worker in the West London Mission of the Methodist Church, and wrote of her conversion to the "gospel of socialism as it was preached in our day by Keir Hardie in the political field, and by Edward Carpenter as a philosopher and a poet".[48] In *A Life's Work* (1949), Margaret Bondfield, the first woman to achieve cabinet rank as Minister of Labour in Ramsay MacDonald's government (1929–31), tells how the Christian activism of her family helped her own political formation—one brother was an officer in the Salvation Army, another a missionary in China, and her sister became a Wesleyan deaconess.[49]

The early campaigns of the women's suffragette movement bore a striking resemblance to the religious revivalist movements of late Victorian Britain. Emmeline Pankhurst writes: "We adopted Salvation Army Methods and went out into the highways and the byways after Converts"; she adds: "Just as the Booths and their followers took religion to the street crowds in such fashion that church people were horrified, so we took suffrage to the general public in a manner that amazed and scandalized the other suffragists".[50]

The autobiographers draw freely on the rhetoric and language of Christianity and the Bible: "Roughness we certainly met with. Ours was not a popular cause and at many a meeting we risked life and limb; like St Paul, 'we fought with beasts at Ephesus'", remarks Margaret Wynne Nevinson, a member of the Church League for Women's Suffrage.[51] Edith Picton-Turbevill, a missionary in India until ill-health compelled her return to England, was Vice President of the Young Women's Christian Association and its Director of Appeals. She preached in public and campaigned for women to enter the ministry before being elected Labour Member of Parliament for the Wrekin in Shropshire (1929–31). In *Life Is Good* (1939), Picton-Turbevill recalls her one meeting with Emmeline Pankhurst in 1912, the purpose of which was to urge her to abandon her militant methods. She "quoted the Bible which Mrs Pankhurst also did and quite as effectively. Looking back I think it was something of an impertinence on my part".[52]

What differentiated the suffragettes, in the main, from the constitutional suffragists was their first-hand experience of imprisonment. The suffragette arson campaign and attacks on commercial and private property also generated deep divisions between suffragettes. The *Roll of Honour* of suffrage prisoners lists some thousand persons (overwhelmingly female) estimated to have gone to prison between the start of militant activity in 1905 until its suspension on the outbreak of the First World War.[53] Suffragette prisoners constituted the largest contingent of women ever to have been sent to prison for reasons related to political principle on the British mainland. The precise number of those who went on hunger strike and/or were subjected to forcible feeding while in custody is unknown.

In The Body in Pain: The Making and Unmaking of the World, Elaine Scarry reflects on how physical pain, in contrast to other states of consciousness, is resistant to objectification in language. Such pain is for "the individual experiencing it overwhelmingly present, more emphatically real than any other human experience, and yet is almost invisible to anyone else, unfelt and unknown".[54] *The Body in Pain* explores how political regimes have inflicted pain as an instrument in breaking down or "unmaking" the sufferer's sense of self. In The Cultural Politics of Emotion Sarah Ahmed contends that the impossibility of inhabiting the other's body creates the desire to "know what it feels like". Ahmed terms the latter the "sociality of pain."[55]

If forcible feeding—a procedure widely denounced at the time because women were forced to undergo it without proper nutritional or medical justification—is an attempt on the part of the authorities to "unmake" a resistant ego and to remake this into a more pliant (and compliant) one, the suffragette autobiography is a "reverse discourse". It is the written testimony of a survivor —the discursive attempt to textually refashion the sufferer's sense of self. Suffragette autobiographies *do* contain first- and third-person accounts of forcible feeding. Christabel Pankhurst's *Unshackled* (1958), published posthumously from a manuscript found by Grace Roe, describes the forcible feeding of Mary Richardson, Grace Roe and Nellie Hall.[56]

However, the autobiographical subjects do not linger on their own pain, precisely because, as Scarry points out, this is inexpressible. Instead they dwell on the daily tedium, humiliation and iniquities of prison life that made the words "suffragette" and "prison reformer" virtually interchangeable. Annie Kenney reflects that "[t]he people of the future will look with the same horror on these buildings as we look on the dungeons and the black pits of the middle ages", and concludes: "Prison is a peculiar place to live in [...] The imagination must be very vivid to get away from its deadening, soul-destroying atmosphere. It is a death-trap to aspiration and inspiration".[57]

What emerges from the militant autobiographies is the determination that bodily suffering should not be forgotten and that women's pain should be made to count politically. Mary Sophia Allen is initially reticent to describe her own forcible feeding, but does so "to show these modern young women who sneer at 'The suffragette Frumps' something of what we suffered so that they might have their much-vaunted political freedom".[58] Other middle-class women who witnessed women's suffering, as Poor Law guardians or social reformers among the urban poor, often attribute their own conversion to the "cause" to such experiences and see women's suffering in prison as part of the same continuum.

In *My Own Story* (1914), Emmeline Pankhurst recollects being "horrified to see little girls seven and eight years old on their knees scrubbing the cold stones of the long corridors" of the Chorlton workhouse where heavily pregnant women were "doing the hardest kind of work, almost until their babies came into the world [...] These poor, unprotected mothers and their babies I am sure were potent factors in my education as a militant".[59] Later, when "Holloway became a place of horror and torment", Pankhurst was appalled at the "sickening scenes" of violence during the "disgusting and cruel process of forcible feeding [...] I shall never while I live forget the suffering I experienced during the days when those cries were ringing in my ears".[60]

Tactics such as arson, window-breaking and destroying churches and works of art caused deep internal divisions in the movement. However, while suffragette prisoners were being subjected to disproportionate, if not draconian, sentences for relatively inconsequential public order offences, they enjoyed some degree of public sympathy. Criticism of suffragette violence was often suspended voluntarily (or muted) in suffrage circles as a measure of respect for the women suffering in prison. Sylvia Pankhurst, who had been imprisoned and force-fed many times, explained her own position in her autobiography published in 1931, long after the vote was won and constraints on criticism of the militants no longer operated: "I would not advocate secret militancy. I would take no part in it, but repudiation I would leave to others".[61]

Millicent Garrett Fawcett's feelings on violence were unequivocal. In *What I Remember* (1924), she writes: "To put the whole matter in a sentence, we were convinced that our job was to win the hearts and minds of our countrymen to the justice of our cause, and this could never be done by force and violence".[62] Yet Fawcett refused to be drawn into condemnation of individual acts of violence, consistently pointing to the iniquities of the prison sentences and what women shared in common rather than their differences in her public utterances, and acting with what Maude Royden recollects as "complete reasonableness and a quiet spirit".[63]

Helena Swanwick, a lifelong pacifist, is an exception to the rule. Driven by her commitment to freedom of expression and the "wholesomeness of criticism", Swanwick resigned as editor of the *Common Cause* because "the things I wanted to say about W.S.P.U were such as apparently the N.U would not tolerate in its organ".[64] Swanwick was forthright in her condemnation: "I have never been able to see that it does the cause of women's suffrage any good to refrain from criticizing militant suffragists who, in my opinion, are doing considerable immediate and far more considerable ultimate harm".[65]

In learning how to counter anti-suffragist "physical force" arguments (only those able to defend their country by bearing arms [men] should be entitled to vote), women had developed alternative notions of citizenship based on peace, non-violence and cooperation. Many saw support for war in any form as a violation of fundamental suffragist and democratic principles. Thus, what Fawcett terms in *What I Remember* as her call to all suffragists to "aid our country to the utmost by devising and carrying out well-thought out plans of national usefulness" proved anathema to many of her supporters and led to a sizeable number of resignations from the NUWSS.[66]

The autobiographies of Helena Swanwick, Evelyn Sharp and Emmeline Pethick-Lawrence are richly informative about a little-known aspect of suffrage history: the principled opposition of sizeable sections of the movement to militarism. They also tell us much about what June Purvis describes as the "maternal, imperial feminism" of Emmeline Pankhurst that "gave high priority to women's role in raising the moral tone of the nation and Empire".[67] Women's peace initiatives included the campaigns for a negotiated end to the First World War and to establish the League of Nations as an international peacekeeping organization. Swanwick and Sharp were prevented by the government from attending the Women's Peace Conference at The Hague in 1915. Pethick-Lawrence was one of only three British women who attended, having entered the Netherlands with the United States delegation. Sharp joined the Women's International League for Peace and Freedom, set up to link feminism and the peace movement; Swanwick became Chairman and Emmeline Pethick-Lawrence Treasurer of the British section. In *Unfinished Adventure* (1933), Sharp tells of how she kept the suffrage cause alive "lest, when the time came for dealing with franchise reforms, as it inevitably must come after such a war, the woman's claims should be as usual ignored".[68] Withholding her taxes, she was declared bankrupt and her property was sent to auction: "no ostracism I ever suffered in the militant years was comparable to the misery of being in the minority during the four years of the war".[69]

Autobiographical subjects frequently use the techniques of the novelist—dramatic incident, suspense, foreshadowing, figurative language, character development, etc.—as well as the linear, chronological plot to engage their readers' interest. While the autobiographer purports to tell the life story of a "real" person, the distinction between autobiographical writing and fiction is not clear-cut. Indeed, Virginia Woolf wrote that:

> [...] of all literature (yes, I think this is more or less true) I love autobiography most. In fact, I sometimes think only autobiography is literature—novels are what we peel off, and come at last to the core, which is only you or me.[70]

Yet for all the arguments about autobiography as a literary genre, its specificity as a discursive medium is inseparable from its truth claims. However, the problem of looking to autobiography for the "truth" is that human memory is unreliable and autobiographical disclosure selective; autobiographical subjects almost invariably wish to present themselves in the best possible light. The relationship between the autobiographer and her reader is therefore "crucial to the process of 'composure' by which a narrator produces a story of themselves with which they can live in relative psychic comfort".[71]

All the autobiographers are partial in what they choose to reveal. Millicent Garrett Fawcett, for instance, inexplicably says nothing about the birth of her beloved daughter, Philippa. Sylvia Pankhurst omits any reference to her long love affair with the married Keir Hardie from her autobiography in order to safeguard her privacy. Emmeline Pankhurst's *My Own Story* mentions perfunctorily Emmeline Pethick-Lawrence, who was very important in the early days of the WSPU, and key workers such as Mary Gawthorpe and Dora Montefiore, who subsequently left or were expelled from the WSPU, are omitted. The truth claims of Mary Richardson's *Laugh a Defiance* (1953) are dubious.[72] As Hilda Kean points out, Richardson, a militant who achieved some notoriety for slashing the *Rokeby Venus* in the National Gallery in 1913, situates her personal narrative in the context of the Edwardian suffragette movement, which she deemed acceptable to her first readers, deliberately omitting any mention of her more recent involvement as head of the Women's Section of the British Union of Fascists, which was not.[73] The autobiography also forwards the fictitious claim that Richardson was present at the Derby at Emily Wilding's death; no external corroboration exists, and her presence is not mentioned in either the suffragette or national press coverage. Emphasizing Richardson's unreliability as a narrator, Elizabeth Crawford suggests that she has exaggerated her own importance and her account is not chronologically accurate: "rather she presents a series of incidents, in each of which she takes a starring role. I have little doubt that the purpose of *Laugh a Defiance* was to raise funds".[74]

Winifred Holtby, aged 16 when militancy was suspended in 1914 and too young to have been fully involved, provides this memorable description of its long-term significance:

> It had disproved those ideas about their own nature which were—and sometimes are—among their gravest handicaps. This was the great value of militancy. It broke down hitherto infrangible tabus [...] The very recklessness and extremism of militancy had shaken old certainties. An emotional earthquake had shattered the intangible yet suffocating prison of decorum.[75]

Emmeline Pethick-Lawrence makes much the same point: the militant struggle had produced a "change in the character no less than in the status of women", destroying the "maiming subserviency" that "had for ages held the spirit of the mass of women in thrall", not only for "women actively engaged in the struggle, but for the millions who from afar looked on with critical amazement".[76]

As we have seen, participants in the suffrage campaigns frequently felt that their lives had been radically transformed for the better. But this was often at the cost of damage to their mental and physical health, marital breakdown, severance from family and friends, and deferment or loss of job prospects. In *Female Pipings in Eden* (1933), the composer Ethel Smyth recollects "countless poor women of the working class, nurses, typists, shop girls, and the like, who had good reason to doubt whether their employers would ever take them back again in Holloway Prison".[77] The suffrage autobiographers were aware of a younger generation of women who knew little of recent history and regarded the suffrage campaigns as passé. Their memoirs acknowledge the danger of the vote being divorced from the struggle which had made it possible and the personal sacrifices this struggle had entailed.[78]

Leigh Gilmore suggests that "even in the narrowest and most ambivalent sense, writing an autobiography can be a political act because it asserts a right to speak rather than to be spoken for".[79] Because women's lives have been misrepresented, erased or marginalized within patriarchal societies, autobiographical inscription, which privileges individual subjectivity, is one way of writing women back into the historical record—of changing women from the objects to the subjects of discourse. As Linda Anderson puts it:

> [...] the woman who attempts to write herself is engaged by the nature of the activity itself in re-writing stories that already exist about her [...] She is resisting or changing what is known about her. Her place within culture, the place from which she writes, is produced by difference and produces difference.[80]

The personal voice that speaks beyond itself in these life writings helps the historian not only to reconstitute women's lives at a pivotal moment of historical change, but also to reconfigure the social, cultural and political dimensions of those lives. Women's engagement in public politics therefore comes to be seen not as an atypical or aberrant activity, but on a continuum, as an extension of women's workaday lives. Because the vast majority of women had to renegotiate personal, workplace and domestic relationships before, alongside and after their work for women's suffrage, Sandra Stanley Holton suggests that the autobiographies intimate the

> [...] need to rethink the present organisation of British women's history in this period, an organisation which tends to treat the history of women's involvement with formal politics as a largely separate and discrete area of study from, say, the history of sexuality and reproduction, or of domestic life.[81]

After the war, many suffragists and suffragettes joined feminist organizations such as the Six Point Group, started by Lady Rhondda in 1921, or enjoyed new opportunities for women which were made possible by the acquisition of the vote. The autobiographers acknowledge the "singularity in alternity" of their own achievements—their indebtedness to the women who went before them.[82] Like many veterans, Edith Picton-Turbevill was present at both the unveiling of the statue of Emmeline Pankhurst by Stanley Baldwin in Victoria Tower Gardens in 1930 and the dedication of the medallion in Westminster Abbey in memory of Millicent Garrett Fawcett in 1932. "On one point I do feel confident", she writes: "I would never have had the interesting and absorbing experience of being a Member of Parliament had it not been for the work of these two gallant women".[83]

Notes

1. These are written by Annie Barnes, Margaret Bondfield, Garrett Fawcett, Mary Gawthorpe, Cicely Hamilton, Violet Hunt, Annie Kenney, Hannah Mitchell, Dora Montefiore, Molly Murphy, Margaret Wynne Nevinson, Christabel, Emmeline and Sylvia Pankhurst, Emmeline Pethick-Lawrence, Edith Picton-Turbevill, Mary Richardson, Maude Royden, Maud Arncliffe Sennett, Evelyn Sharp, Ethel Smyth, Helena Swanwick and Margaret Haig Thomas.
2. Note that the Women's Freedom League did not condone arson or damage to property.
3. Margaret Cavendish, Duchess of Newcastle, "Memoirs of Margaret, Duchess of Newcastle", *Life of the First Duke of Newcastle and Other Writing* (1656; London: Dent, 1915), pp. 187–213 (213).
4. Helena Swanwick, *I Have Been Young* (London: Gollancz, 1935), p. 15.
5. Sandra Stanley Holton, "The Making of Suffrage History", *Votes for Women*, ed. June Purvis and Sandra Stanley Holton (London: Routledge, 2000), pp. 13–33 (21).
6. Sidonie Smith, *A Poetics of Women's Autobiography: Marginality and the Fictions of Self-Representation* (Bloomington: Indiana UP, 1987), p. 48.
7. Maude Royden, "A. Maude Royden", *Myself When Young*, ed. Margaret Oxford (London: Muller, 1938), pp. 361–82 (381).
8. Maroula Joannou, "'Who Would Be Politically Free Herself Must Strike the Blow': Suffragette Autobiography and Suffragette Militancy", *The Uses of Autobiography*, ed. Julia Swindells (London: Taylor and Francis, 1995), pp. 31–44 (31).
9. For an analysis of the autobiographies of Christabel, Emmeline and Sylvia Pankhurst which refutes the notion that *My Own Story* was "ghostwritten" and addresses the sibling relationships between Sylvia and Christabel, see Maureen Wright and June Purvis, "Writing Suffragette History: The Contending Autobiographical Narratives of the Pankhursts", *Women's History Review*, 14.3–4 (2005): 405–33.
10. Laura E. Nym Mayhall, "Creating the 'Suffragette Spirit': British Feminism and the Historical Imagination", *Women's History Review*, 4.3 (1995): 319–44.
11. Leigh Gilmore, *Autobiographics: A Feminist Theory of Women's Self-Representation* (Ithaca, NY: Cornell UP, 1994), p. 109.
12. James Olney, "'I Was Born': Slave Narratives, Their Status as Autobiography and as Literature", *Callaloo*, 20 (1984): 46–73 (47).

13. Tess Cosslett, Celia Lury, and Penny Summerfield, introduction, *Feminism and Autobiography: Texts, Theories Methods*, ed. Cosslett, Lury, and Summerfield (London: Routledge, 2000), pp. 1–21 (4).
14. Evelyn Sharp, *Unfinished Adventure: Selected Reminiscences from an Englishwomen's Life* (London: John Lane, 1934), p. 136.
15. Annie Kenney, *Memories of a Militant* (London: Edward Arnold, 1924), p. 289.
16. Bella Brodski and Celeste Schenck, eds., *Life/Lines: Theorizing Women's Autobiography* (Ithaca, NY: Cornell UP, 1988), p. 11.
17. Millicent Garrett Fawcett, *Women's Suffrage: A Short History of a Great Movement* (London: T. C. and E. C. Jack, 1912), pp. 61–62.
18. Andrew Rosen, *Rise Up Women: The Militant Campaign of the Women's Social and Political Union 1903–1914* (London: Routledge, 1974), p. 92.
19. Sandra Stanley Holton, *Suffrage Days: Stories from the Women's Suffrage Movement* (London: Routledge, 1996), p. 35.
20. Cicely Hamilton, *Life Errant* (London: Dent, 1935), p. 66.
21. Dora Montefiore, *From a Victorian to a Modern* (London: E. Archer, 1927), p. 108.
22. Margaret Wynne Nevinson, *Life's Fitful Fever: A Volume of Memories* (London: A. and C. Black, 1926), p. 192.
23. Maud Arncliffe Sennett, *The Child: The Writer's Experience of the Woman's Suffrage Movement, 1906–18* (London: C. W. Daniels, 1938), p. 58.
24. Sennett, p. 58.
25. "Letter from Jane Sharp to Evelyn Sharp", n.d.; qtd. in Angela John, *Evelyn Sharp, Rebel Woman, 1869–1955* (Manchester: Manchester UP, 2009), p. 65. The reference to the second division is to the category below that of political prisoner, which had more privileges. Suffragettes lobbied to be recognized as political prisoners who were in the first division.
26. Violet Hunt, *The Flurried Years* (London: Hurst and Blackett, 1926), p. 42.
27. Annie Barnes, *Tough Annie: From Suffragette to Stepney Councillor* (London: Stepney Books, 1980), p. 15.
28. Mary S. Allen, *Lady in Blue* (London: Stanley Paul, 1936), p. 14.
29. Swanwick, pp. 81, 138.
30. Hamilton, p. 65.
31. Liz Stanley, *The Auto/biographical I: The Theory and Practice of Feminist Auto/biography* (Manchester: Manchester UP, 1992), p. 252.
32. Hamilton, p. 65.
33. Royden, p. 381.
34. Barnes, p. 18.
35. Margaret, Lady Rhondda, *This Was My World* (London: Macmillan, 1933), p. 120.
36. Kathryn Dodd, introduction, *A Sylvia Pankhurst Reader*, ed. Dodd (Manchester: Manchester UP, 1993), p. 15.
37. Rhondda, p. 162.
38. Nevinson, p. 212.
39. Nevinson, p. 213.
40. Nevinson, p. 212.
41. Violet Hunt, *The Flurried Years* (London: Hurst and Blackett, 1926), p. 42.
42. Molly Murphy, *Molly Murphy: Suffragette and Socialist* (Salford: Inst. of Social Research, U of Salford, 1998), p. 7.

43. Mary Gawthorpe, *Up Hill to Holloway* (Penobscote, ME: Traversity, 1962), pp. 173, 180.
44. Kenney, p. 110.
45. Hannah Mitchell, *The Hard Way Up: Autobiography of Hannah Mitchell, Suffragette and Rebel*, ed. Geoffrey Mitchell (London: Faber, 1977), p. 130. This expression is used for the title of Jill Liddington and Jill Norris's *One Hand Tied Behind Us: The Rise of the Women's Suffrage Movement* (London: Virago, 1978).
46. Swanwick, p.187
47. Lesley Parker Hume, *The National Union of Women's Suffrage Societies, 1897–1914* (New York: Garland, 1982), p. 12.
48. Emmeline Pethick-Lawrence, *My Part in a Changing World* (London: Gollancz, 1938), p. 75.
49. Margaret Bondfield, *A Life's Work* (London: Hutchinson, 1949), pp. 18–19.
50. Emmeline Pankhurst, *My Own Story* (London: Everleigh Nash, 1914), p. 62.
51. Nevinson, p. 212.
52. Edith Picton-Turbevill, *Life Is Good: An Autobiography* (London: Morgan and Scott, 1939), p. 110.
53. *Roll of Honour, Suffragette Prisoners 1905–1914* (Keighley: Rydal, n.d.)
54. Elaine Scarry, *The Body in Pain: The Making and Unmaking of the World* (Oxford: Oxford UP, 1985), p.5.
55. Sarah Ahmed, The Cultural Politics of Emotion (London Routledge, 2004), p.29, p.28.
56. Frederick Pethick-Lawrence ed., Christabel Pankhurst, *Unshackled: the Story of How* We Won the Vote, by Christabel Pankhurst (London: Hutchinson, 1958), p. 285.
57. Kenney, p. 97.
58. Allen, p. 21.
59. E. Pankhurst, pp. 25, 28.
60. E. Pankhurst, pp. 251, 252.
61. Sylvia Pankhurst, *The Suffragette Movement: An Intimate Account of Persons and Ideals* (London: Longman, 1931), p. 402.
62. Millicent Garrett Fawcett, *What I Remember* (London: Fisher Unwin, 1924), p. 192.
63. Royden, p. 382.
64. Swanwick, pp. 231, 223.
65. Swanwick, p. 231.
66. Fawcett, *What*, p. 219.
67. June Purvis, *Emmeline Pankhurst: A Biography* (London: Routledge, 2002), p. 338.
68. Sharp, p. 157.
69. Sharp, p. 161.
70. Virginia Woolf, "Letter to Hugh Walpole Dated December 28 1932", *The Letters of Virginia Woolf, Volume 5: The Sickle Side of the Moon, 1932–35*, ed. Nigel Nicolson and Joanne Trautmann (London: Chatto, 1979), pp. 141–42 (142).
71. Cosslett, Lury, and Summerfield, p. 3.
72. Mary Richardson, *Laugh a Defiance* (London: Weidenfeld and Nicolson, 1953).
73. Hilda Kean, "Some Problems of Constructing and Reconstructing a Suffragette's Life: Mary Richardson, Suffragette, Socialist and Fascist", *Women's History Review*, 7.4 (1998): 475–93 (476).

74. Elizabeth Crawford, "What Links Charles Dickens, the Rokeby Venus and the Number 38 Bus?" *Woman and Her Sphere*, 4 Jan. 2017 <https://womanandhersphere.com/2014/06/23/suffrage-stories-what-links-charles-dickens-the-rokeby-venus-and-the-number-38-bus/>.
75. Winifred Holtby, *Women in a Changing Civilization* (London: John Lane, 1934), pp. 52–53.
76. Pethick-Lawrence, *My Part*, p. 239.
77. Ethel Smyth, *Female Pipings in Eden* (London: Peter Davies, 1934), p. 211.
78. See Hilda Kean, "Searching for the Past in Present Defeat: The Construction of Historical and Political Identity in British Feminism in the 1920s and 1930s", *Women's History Review*, 3.1 (1994): 57–80 (60).
79. Gilmore, p. 40.
80. Linda Anderson, "At the Threshold of the Self", *Women's Writing: A Challenge to Theory*, ed. Moira Monteith (Brighton: Harvester, 1986), pp. 54–71 (59).
81. Sandra Stanley Holton, "The Suffragist and the 'Average Woman'", *Women's History Review*, 1.1 (1992): 9–24 (10).
82. Brodski and Schenck, p. 11.
83. Picton-Turbevill, pp. 111–12.

Disclosure statement

No potential conflict of interest was reported by the author.

"WOMEN WHO DARED TO ASK FOR A VOTE": THE MISSING MEMOIRS OF THE SCOTTISH SUFFRAGETTES

Gemma Elliott

ABSTRACT
In an area of political history as under-represented as women's fight for their right to vote, the involvement of Scotland's suffrage campaigners is even less known, researched and discussed. These women contributed greatly to the cause, taking part in just as much militant activism as their London-based peers, but their stories have not received recognition in the same way. Some Scottish suffrage campaigners did seek to have their voices heard by writing first-person memoirs on their struggles, but these have largely gone unpublished and unnoticed. This article discusses the fascinating lives and autobiographies of two Scottish Women's Social and Political Union members, Elizabeth Thomson and Jessie Stephen, and questions why their fascinating stories have remained hidden away in inaccessible archives for so long.

If women's fight for the vote in Britain has been under-represented in history, then the involvement of Scottish women has suffered even more. Suffrage historian Leah Leneman addressed this in the introduction to her monograph *A Guid Cause: The Women's Suffrage Movement in Scotland*, stating that this element of women's history has been told "almost exclusively from the point of view of the metropolitan leadership".[1] However, Scottish women, and women living in Scotland, were just as politically active and just as important to the cause as their London-based counterparts, which Leneman has tried to make known. It seems that what is missing from the history of the campaign for women's suffrage in Scotland are the stories of the women themselves, which Leneman addresses in *The Scottish Suffragettes*:

> The point is that those women [Scottish suffrage campaigners] did not seek attention for themselves. Emmeline, Christabel and Sylvia Pankhurst were charismatic figures in "The Suffragette Movement", as Sylvia called it. They produced autobiographies centred on their personal involvement and naturally their close acolytes were also included in the story; but the lively, articulate campaigners elsewhere in England, and in Scotland and Wales, without whom the whole thing would have gone nowhere, barely got a mention.[2]

However, what Leneman fails to note is that Scottish women fighting for suffrage did record their own history and write their own lives; their stories have just received very limited recognition.

British suffrage autobiographies have attracted some critical attention in recent years, although the focus has predominantly been on the writings of those within the middle-class, London-based campaign groups such as the Pankhursts' Women's Social and Political Union (WSPU). Hilda Kean, in an article on Canadian-born suffrage campaigner and WSPU member Mary Richardson, discusses the large number of memoirs which were written by women involved in the suffrage movement as a method of forming their own identities within their political groups, noting that these women "constructed their own identities through public activities and autobiographical writing".[3] Maroula Joannou also discusses this focus on the personal in memoirs of suffragettes, stating that "the focus on individual subjectivity in suffragette autobiography involves the construction of a personal identity in which investment in the communal is at least as strong as investment in the individualistic".[4] Here, Joannou and Kean use the same language of the construction of selfhood to describe the life writing of the suffrage campaigners, suggesting that these women who chose to write memoirs did so with the purpose of defining their own roles within the collective action of the campaign groups. Kean has also noted, in a separate essay on suffrage commemoration, the lengths suffrage campaigners went to not only to record their histories, but also to preserve them for future study, working as their own historians: "In the suffrage context the role of the militant suffrage feminists themselves, as public historians, collecting, preserving—and displaying —the material culture of the movement, needs to be recognised. The suffragettes contributed to their own historical survival".[5] In an article on the autobiographical writings of Christabel, Emmeline and Sylvia Pankhurst, June Purvis and Maureen Wright have also discussed this idea of suffragettes as active historians of their own campaigns, noting that the memoirs of these three women, amongst the most recognized names within women's history, are vital historical resources, despite their personal biases:

> Emmeline, Christabel and Sylvia Pankhurst were all participants in, as well as chroniclers of, the suffragette movement. Their narratives collapse the boundaries so many have constructed between so-called "objective" history, as told by a third person narrator, and the "subjective" story of the autobiographer. Yet histories are subjective and laden with values, and autobiographies are history for their authors. All three Pankhurst women positioned themselves in both the individual context of the part each believed she played within the suffragette movement, as well as within the broader, general context of the campaign.[6]

Sylvia Pankhurst's autobiographical writing was also considered useful at the time of its production, with Krista Cowman explaining in an article on suffrage campaigner Mary Gawthorpe that Pankhurst's texts could be used as something of a guide to grass-roots campaigning for younger recruits:

> Pankhurst's autobiographical perspective helped Gawthorpe, a slightly late entrant into the WSPU, make sense of some of her own experiences. Unlike Annie Kenney, the other prominent working-class leader with whom she is frequently compared, Gawthorpe had had no direct experience of the genesis of the WSPU prior to its adoption of militancy. Nor, despite sharing the Independent Labour Party (ILP) background of the Pankhurst family, did she have personal knowledge of the radical politics of Lancashire before her appointment as Manchester organiser, having been born and bred in Leeds. Engaging with the WSPU after its move to London must have provoked many queries for its new organiser which the speed and intensity of the campaign gave no opportunity to investigate.[7]

However, Laura E. Nym Mayhall critiques this preoccupation with the Pankhursts and with the WSPU, claiming that current feminist writing focuses too closely on their contribution: "what all these interpretations share is a belief in the centrality of the suffragette experience as told from one perspective—that of the Women's Social and Political Union under the leadership of Emmeline and Christabel Pankhurst".[8] The suffragette experience and the urge to record their histories as they were happening, however, was not limited to the Pankhursts and other middle-class English campaigners who remain well-known names of women's history. Suffrage campaigners from outside of this metropolitan and elite mainstream also wrote autobiographies detailing fascinating lives of political activism, with many of these remaining unpublished and inaccessible in archives. This article looks at just two of these, written by Elizabeth Thomson and Jessie Stephen.

Elizabeth Thomson and Jessie Stephen were both members of Scottish branches of the WSPU in the early years of the twentieth century. With Thomson based in Edinburgh and Stephen in Glasgow, there is no evidence that the two met or campaigned together, but they are linked in their urge to write down their experiences of political activism, with both women having produced first-person memoirs. Thomson's unpublished autobiography is held in the University of Glasgow's Archive Services,[9] and Stephen's, which is also unpublished, can be found in Manchester's Working Class Movement Library.[10] Published approximately five decades apart, the two memoirs differ greatly in their tone and content, with Thomson's written during her years as an active campaigner, whilst Stephen's comes some years after universal suffrage has been achieved. Stephen's memoir is also intensely personal, while Thomson at times combines her own life story with that of her sister. However, both are similar in that they cover almost the entire lives of their writers, and therefore the time spent campaigning for women's suffrage is just one element described in the lives of activism that these two women led. This then differentiates the memoirs from the more well-known suffrage autobiographical texts, such as those written by the Pankhursts, in that their focus has not solely been on campaigning, but rather it forms just one important part of a wider life story.

In the interview with popular feminist magazine *Spare Rib* for which Jessie Stephen is possibly best known, she complains that books on women's history do not represent her experience of the suffrage campaign as it really was:

> There was a lot more than the vote. You see, most of these books—I've read a good few of them at different times—they don't really go very deep. They don't talk about the discussions we used to have, the aspirations the ordinary member of the W.S.P.U. was thinking about. These were about jobs, about wages, about the present matrimonial laws. All that sort of thing used to be discussed by us. I didn't know a lot about it, but some of these women did.[11]

What Stephen does not mention here is that her memoir, "Submission Is for Slaves", along with Elizabeth Thomson's "The Life Story of Miss Elizabeth Thomson" are the stories which do go deeper and address these omissions. Here, Stephen's claim that most texts on women's history focus only on the campaign for suffrage, and fail to discuss the whole host of other problems women have faced, is a vital one. She makes a case for including memoirs like her own and Elizabeth Thomson's, which do cover a variety of issues and which show the real diversity of ages and social classes involved in the suffrage campaign, in the wider discussion on women's political histories.

Elizabeth Thomson, born in Glasgow in 1847, is an unusual figure in the suffrage movement as she was in her sixties when she first became interested in campaigning and indeed became involved in violent militant action, despite her age. Her father, Robert Dundas Thomson, graduated from the University of Glasgow in 1831 with a medical degree, and her maternal grandfather, Thomas Thomson, was Regius Professor of Chemistry at the university from 1818 to 1852. Her memoir, presumably held in the University of Glasgow's archives due to her father and grandfather's connections, describes how, following her grandfather's death in 1852, Thomson and her family moved to London, where she spent the remainder of her childhood. Much of Thomson's unpublished autobiography details her time travelling the world, and she often draws attention to the work that she observed of women, although her feminism is not explicitly stated.

In 1879, Thomson was treated by Sophia Jex-Blake, the first practising female doctor in Scotland and a feminist campaigner. Speaking of this encounter in her autobiography, Thomson states: "On my return to Edinburgh I saw Dr. Jex Blake who had just completed her study at Zurich and settled in Manor Place. She kept me lying down all winter, and in the next summer '80 I was better".[12] Thomson seems to have deliberately sought out female doctors, of whom there were very few at the time, as she also mentions being treated by Elizabeth Garrett Anderson, the sister of Millicent Garrett

Fawcett, president of the National Union of Women's Suffrage Societies. Anderson was the first English woman to qualify as a doctor, and Thomson claims that she "cured me after a few weeks treatment".[13] Thomson also writes about a Dr Caroline Sturge, who treated a foot injury she suffered in 1897.

Throughout the 1890s and 1900s, Thomson travelled with her sister Agnes, with both of them working as teachers and missionaries. They visited India, Japan, the USA, Germany and Italy, amongst many other countries, returning to the UK, via Vienna, Prague, Dresden and Berlin, in 1909 to settle in Edinburgh.

In June 1909, aged 61, Thomson saw women's suffrage campaigner Emmeline Pankhurst, leader of the WSPU, speak at Synod Hall in Edinburgh. She was motivated by this speech, along with her sister, to join the WSPU, and noted that Pankhurst's stories of hardship in prison had influenced their decision: "we were horrified, and made up our minds to join the W.S.P.U. at once".[14] In October 1909, a large protest for women's suffrage took place in Edinburgh, with a march along Princes Street, which Thomson describes in her memoir as "well arranged" but "rowdy".[15] In 1910, Thomson and her sister travelled to London to join the Pankhursts in their increasingly physical, and at times violent, fight for women's suffrage. On 18 November 1910, the infamous clash between suffrage campaigners and police officers, known as Black Friday, took place on the streets of London. Thomson describes this day, noting that she was hurt by a man hitting her in the back, but that the other women involved were "so careful not to hurt each other" in the crush of bodies, exemplifying the solidarity of the movement.[16] Thomson continued to campaign for the WSPU in London, despite her age and the violence involved. In 1911, she was held at Cannon Row police station for throwing stones at government buildings. She explains that "1911 was our first experience of the hatred of the Government to women who dared to ask for a vote"[17]—presumably the source of the anger that led her to participate in the destruction of property. In 1912, she was imprisoned in Holloway gaol for one month for her part in a suffrage protest.

In 1912 and 1913, Thomson travelled in Scandinavia, returning to Edinburgh in 1913 where her WSPU efforts continued. On 19 May 1913, aged 65, she went on trial at Jedburgh, Edinburgh, for her part in the attempted arson at Kelso racecourse on 5 April of the same year. She was tried alongside her sister Agnes and two other well-known Scottish suffrage campaigners, Arabella Scott and Edith Hudson. Thomson was sentenced to three months in Calton Prison, but took part in a hunger strike, which led to her early release under the Cat and Mouse Act. On 31 May, against court orders, Thomson fled Edinburgh for Germany. Edinburgh court records from 1913, held in the National Records of Scotland, show that on 27 May the police claimed to "of course know where they [Thomson and Arabella

Scott] are living", but they admitted on 13 June 1913 that "the police have no information to the present whereabouts of Elizabeth Thomson and Edith Hudson and are continuing their search for them".[18] The police did not find Thomson and she spent the winter of 1913 in San Sebastian, Spain, before travelling to London in May 1914. Thomson died at her home in Edinburgh on 12 March 1918.[19]

Elizabeth Thomson is not a well-known figure of the Scottish suffrage movement. The only mention of her in Leneman's *A Guid Cause* is in reference to the attempted arson at Kelso racecourse, which also involved Edith Hudson and Arabella Scott, who are more frequently associated with the movement in Scotland. Leneman describes Elizabeth and her sister Agnes as "hardly the stereotype young WSPU militants", noting their ages of 65 and 67, respectively, at the time of their arrests.[20] This reinforces the unusual nature of their campaigning, but also suggests that the Thomsons were notable for nothing more than their age, rather than as the tireless and militant campaigners that they were. Elizabeth Crawford is also guilty of this, referring to the women as "two elderly sisters".[21] As Thomson's memoir has never been published, it is mainly accessible just to the academic community and to those who know where to look and what to search for in online archival records. Because of this, the only information on her life of international travel and militant activism is these brief mentions in connection to the Kelso racecourse incident, meaning that little information about Thomson, other than her advanced age, can be accessed by the wider public.

Jessie Stephen is far better known than Thomson. This is due in part to her lifelong dedication to campaigning for trade unions and her 1922 election as a Labour councillor, but also thanks to her aforementioned 1975 interview with *Spare Rib*, where she discusses everything from her political ambitions to helping her mother with matters of birth control. Stephen's socialist politics, derived from her working-class background, make her an interesting figure in the women's suffrage movement as the two forms of political activism were often thought to be incompatible. June Hannam and Karen Hunt, in their book *Socialist Women: Britain, 1880s to 1920s*, note that there was a "fragility of any possible alliance, let alone identity, between the two movements" of socialism and suffrage, and discuss how the WSPU, itself formed in conjunction with the Independent Labour Party, split from the left-wing party with some fearing that "suffrage had made mischief in the ranks of socialism".[22] Thus, Stephen's negotiation of her conflicting identities as working-class socialist and militant suffragette means that she should be considered as significant for adding a different dimension to our understanding of the campaign for women's suffrage.

Like Thomson, Stephen, born in 1894, starts her memoir from childhood, crediting her early upbringing for her political leanings: "I know with certainty that my innate urge to rebellion against the injustices of our society were fostered and encouraged by my father".[23] Her father was a member of the Independent Labour Party and enrolled his children in Socialist Sunday School, with Stephen noting that: "what we learned there was in no way inferior to the ethics taught elsewhere".[24] Stephen had aspirations of attending university, but the financial situation of her family forced her instead to go into full-time employment in domestic service. It was during her time in domestic service that she began to embrace fully her need to participate in politics, inspired by the low pay which domestic servants received and the poor conditions in which many were expected to live. Stephen enlisted other maids from properties nearby and set up the Scottish Domestic Workers' Federation.

Around the same time as her involvement in union activities was beginning, Stephen also became interested in the fight for women's voting rights and joined a Glasgow branch of the WSPU. She notes in her autobiography the great variety of fellow suffrage campaigners who had joined her group:

> We had established a group in Glasgow in which there was a very mixed membership indeed, there were ladies who came from wealthy families, there were the ordinary middle class section, usually the intellectuals, and there was a fair scraping too of socialist and ordinary working women.[25]

Stephen goes into detail about the campaign activity for which she is best known: the destruction of mail in post boxes with acid. It is for this action that she is mentioned in the texts of women's history, with Crawford noting that she "took part, surreptitiously, in the militant campaign" by carrying out her destructive activities unnoticed in her domestic servant uniform.[26] Leneman also discusses the postal attacks in *The Scottish Suffragettes*, claiming that "Jessie never encountered suspicion, and had no compunction about carrying out these attacks".[27] Elspeth King's pamphlet *The Scottish Women's Suffrage Movement* mentions Stephen's acid attacks but notes that "few working class women took part in the militant action", marking Stephen out as an anomaly in the movement, despite her own claims that her WSPU branch had a very diverse membership.[28] Discussing the acid attacks in her own words, Stephen writes:

> To my young mind these were exciting times and one of my assignments was the destruction of the contents of a postal pillar box. It was part of a most carefully planned operation to cover the whole city and the timing was perfect. Every member taking part in this had to go out at a certain time and deposit a parcel of acid into the pillar box and walk away unconcernedly leaving the rest to fate. Dressed in my maid's uniform I walked from my place of employment down to the corner of the street where the pillar box stood, dropped in my little package, walked away again and reached home without interruption. This operation was carried out as I have said all over the city and all at the same time, with the result that hundreds of packages were destroyed that evening and not one member of the W .S. & P .U. taking part was caught. Our militancy in Scotland, as in England, took many forms such as the smashing of plate glass

windows, going into art galleries and even attempts to burn down castles and other stately homes.[29]

Stephen's focus on the excitement she felt carrying out these attacks, as well as her seeming pride in how well planned they were, emphasizes her commitment to the militant campaign for women's suffrage at the time. This shows there was space for working-class women in the campaign, despite King's claim that such women were not involved in the Scottish militant action.

Much like Elizabeth Thomson, Stephen portrays her witnessing of Emmeline Pankhurst speaking about the suffrage campaign as an influential moment, particularly since the meeting in Glasgow, as Stephen describes it, was raided by the police and required Pankhurst to hide herself in a laundry basket to evade capture and reimprisonment under the Cat and Mouse Act. Stephen names Pankhurst as "our leader", reinforcing her commitment to the WSPU and to the campaign for women's voting rights.[30] Shortly after this event, Stephen decided to move from Glasgow to London since, as a known political activist, she was finding it difficult to gain employment in Scotland. In England, she worked for the Domestic Workers' Union and then, after a brief return to Scotland, was employed by Sylvia Pankhurst to do organizational work for her Workers' Suffrage Federation (WSF), formerly the East London Federation of Suffragettes. The WSF was formed by Sylvia Pankhurst as a pacifist response to the WSPU and what Crawford describes as "the extremist pro-war stand taken by [Sylvia Pankhurst's] mother and sister".[31]

As early as 1913, there had been a split in the Pankhurst family. While her sister Christabel, a key leader of the WSPU at that time, was concentrating her efforts on raising publicity for the women's suffrage cause, Sylvia had become increasingly involved with the socialist and labour movement, and this change in focus caused tensions within the family. As Barbara Winslow has detailed, Christabel was concerned that Sylvia "was always thinking for herself and acting on her ideas, a trait that made her incompatible with the WSPU".[32] According to Sylvia, Christabel claimed that "a working women's movement was of no value: working women were the weakest portion of the sex: how could it be otherwise? Their lives were too hard, their education too meagre to equip them for the contest".[33] Sylvia and her East London branch were then expelled from the WSPU, which led to the formation of a separate entity: the East London Federation of Suffragettes.

In her memoir, Stephen describes how her first assignment of knocking on doors in Hackney to recruit WSF branch members was dispiriting, with most members of the public she encountered being uninterested. She notes that it "was not an exciting baptism in my new career".[34] It is unsurprising that Jessie Stephen chose to align herself with the far-left politics of the WSF, due to her lifelong association with the Independent Labour Party and her firm socialist views. It is interesting, however, to note that Stephen saw this work with less fortunate sections of society to be just as vital a part of her life as her militant campaigning for the vote, and she spent an equal amount of time discussing both types of activism in her memoir. This, alongside her decision to spend a great deal of her adult life living in England, suggests that perhaps Stephen's outsider status in the history of the women's suffrage movement, with her memoir as yet unpublished and her name not particularly well known, is not in fact due to her Scottish roots, but instead because of her dedication to socialist causes inspired by her own working-class background. Like Sylvia Pankhurst, Stephen's mission to help working-class people separated her from those in organizations such as the WSPU whose only focus was to gain the vote for women. Unlike Sylvia, however, Stephen herself came from a working-class family and struggled with her finances throughout her life. It was not as unusual as one might think for women of Stephen's background to be involved in the suffrage campaign. It was, however, far more difficult for them to participate, and it had a different impact on their lives compared with their middle- and upper-class counterparts, since greater sacrifices had to be made. In their book on the contribution to the suffrage movement of working women from Lancashire, Jill Liddington and Jill Norris note that:

> Middle-class women could always rely on servants to provide their families with regular meals and look after the children. Working-class women had no such safety net, and their absence from home, however brief, revealed how vital was their contribution to the family economy.[35]

Therefore, because of the risks to their families' lives, working-class women tended to participate less in activities which were risky and therefore drew public attention and possible criminal conviction, such as window-breaking. Thus, the efforts of working-class women have not been remembered in the same way as women who had less to lose with regard to their families and finances, and therefore could give more of themselves to the campaign for women's suffrage. Jessie Stephen was a rare exception. As Leneman notes, she is one of the few working-class suffrage campaigners who is somewhat well known while "all but a handful remain in the shadows".[36] Unlike the women to whom family came first, Stephen never married or had children. She gave her entire life to political activism and, in particular, to her attempts to help the working class, as she did with her work for the WSF.

Stephen did go on to enjoy working for the WSF, despite her disappointing beginning knocking on doors, but is not particularly complimentary in her autobiography about Sylvia Pankhurst. She gives various examples of when Sylvia went against committee decisions and claims that "Sylvia Pankhurst could disarm by her charm when she liked, but at the core she was hard as nails and rather inclined to be as autocratic as her mother".[37] Stephen also describes problems encountered due to the ongoing First World War, noting that "the war introduced many complications. Detectives attended all meetings and took shorthand notes of the speeches. Ugly incidents were all part of the hazards of pacifist propaganda".[38] However, Stephen's experience of working at the WSF, while not easy, prepared her for a lifelong career of political campaigning.

In 1917, Stephen left her post at the WSF to work as a political organizer in Bermondsey, south London, for the Independent Labour Party, of which she had been a member since childhood. Having been involved in campaign publicity for several Independent Labour Party by-election candidates, Stephen was elected as a Labour councillor for Bermondsey in 1922 and was made vice-chairperson of the health committee and a member of the housing committee. She stood as a Labour candidate for Portsmouth in several general elections but did not win a seat. In 1944, Stephen was elected Union Area Organiser for Bristol of the National Union of Clerks and, in 1948, she joined the management committee of the Bristol Co-operative Society. In 1957, Stephen was the first female to be elected chair of the Corporate Estates Committee in Bristol. Her memoir ends rather abruptly, with a note on the importance of voluntary political work as a means to "serve their fellow citizens".[39]

Elizabeth Thomson's and Jessie Stephen's unpublished memoirs are quite different in tone and content. Thomson's focuses very much on a straightforward account of the facts of her life, giving many dates and locations to allow the reader to form an accurate timeline. Stephen is instead more concerned with emotions and anecdotes, giving few firm dates but plenty of colourful and personal stories, such as an account of a Canadian man who sent her "the most ardent billet-doux" after a brief encounter.[40] Discussing the autobiography of Mary Richardson, Kean has noted that Richardson's memoir, like others of its kind, does not include such overtly personal and candid writing: "in common with much suffrage autobiography there is very little mention of a life outside a public political domain".[41] This further differentiates Stephen's unpublished autobiography from those which have attracted more critical attention.

Textually, Thomson's autobiography is unusual and interesting, if a little clunky to read, due to her frequent use of the plural pronoun "we" to describe the joint activities of herself and her sister. This is not a common mode of first-person narrative; as the literary critic Uri Margolin notes, it is "so rare" a format, due to the difficulty in portraying "solidarity, unity, distinctness, sharing" in a stylish way.[42] As Margolin puts it: "the payoff may simply not be worth the effort".[43] Perhaps, then, what Thomson's memoir lacks in readability it makes up for in the ambition of its author's attempt to portray the unity and community spirit of the campaign for women's suffrage through her writing style. Furthermore, Thomson's many references to female doctors and professionals feel like an intentional promotion of the important work women were doing. Stephen, too, uses her memoir to promote the women around her, mentioning many female campaigners with whom she interacts or whose work she admires. She also devotes a great deal of her life story to accounts of the poor conditions and inequalities in pay and in treatment which women continued to suffer in the workplace. Thus, it is clear that both Stephen's and Thomson's memoirs are not only fascinating first-person insights into the suffrage campaign, but also provide important records of the history of the fight for women's suffrage in Scotland and of Scottish women campaigning in England. A key difference between the two, however, is their dates of production. Neither has a firm date attached to its archive record, but from the events described, as well as the date of her death, it is clear that Thomson's was completed shortly before she died in 1918. Stephen, on the other hand, who was much younger than Thomson when she took part in the WSPU, recounts many other events in her life over subsequent decades, and it is likely, therefore, that her memoir was not finished until the 1970s. Thus, while Thomson was writing the story of her life as a suffragette during the very time of the struggle, there was a greater distance between the writing of Stephen's memoir and the time when she was campaigning. Her account is therefore more reflective, including both the dull errands of militancy—such as knocking on doors to collect supporters—as well as the dramatically violent incidents.

The close proximity of Thomson's autobiography to the campaigning which it describes, with no time for reflection and contemplation, perhaps goes some way to explaining its somewhat stilted delivery, which makes for an awkward narrative style. It also explains her focus on specific events, such as the Black Friday incidents, rather than the overall outcomes of campaigning. Nonetheless, the immediacy of Thomson's memoir should surely have earned it a place as a vital document of women's history, since it is one of the very few suffrage memoirs written at the time of the campaign, by someone who did not know if the cause they were fighting for would ever be achieved. Although Stephen's memoir was completed much later, at a time when universal suffrage had been agreed and, indeed, she herself had stood for political office, her working-class background, candid writing style and detailed descriptions of militant action suggest that her autobiography should be a vital text in women's political history. Both Stephen's and Thomson's memoirs present, in several different ways, a perspective from outside of the typical suffrage story.

With Thomson's memoir in a university archive rarely visited by those outside of academic institutions, and Stephen's in a niche archive of working-class political memorabilia due to her Independent Labour Party ties, neither are particularly accessible to the wider public, despite the vital importance of the perspectives they provide. Emmeline Pankhurst's *My Own Story* has recently been republished by Penguin with a cover design that ties it to Sarah Gavron' and Abi Morgan's 2015 *Suffragette* film, suggesting it was influential in the writing of the film, as well as that it has the potential to sell copies. Stephen's and Thomson's efforts might be just as insightful as Pankhurst's memoir, and perhaps more interesting as they provide a perspective from outside the mainstream, but it is simply that Emmeline Pankhurst continues to be well known. The problem, then, is that Elizabeth Thomson's and Jessie Stephen's memoirs, as with much of women's personal writings, have only a small readership. Unless this is widened, historical studies will continue to focus on the small group of more well-known suffrage campaigners and their autobiographies.

Deborah Withers has discussed the inaccessibility of women's historical artefacts in her 2015 monograph *Feminism, Digital Culture and the Politics of Transmission*:

> Early on in my engagement with feminist archives, I learnt a key lesson: that the existence and organisation of materials is only one (but of course a crucial) part of the political struggle. If the vast-ness of feminism's already-there is to be accessed and mobilised, they have to be actively and deliberately transmitted.[44]

The "already-there" to which she refers is Withers' term for the generic information on women's history, be it a book or an item in a museum, which is readily available in museums, archives, libraries and even on the Internet. Withers believes that these items cannot be left to be found; they must be, as stated above, "deliberately transmitted". She uses an example of the 1977 proposed sale of the Fawcett Library's collection to the London School of Economics, which was planning to keep only "those parts they deemed important and could enter into the Dewey decimal system and discarding the rest".[45] Although the collection is now known as the Women's Library and has been housed at the London School of Economics since 2013, the purchase was blocked in 1977 by a vote of Fawcett Society members, who chose instead to sell the collection to City Polytechnic, where it could be kept together. This decision by the members suggests that the Dewey classification system, which has fixed and limited classes in which to categorize material, was not flexible enough to house much of the collection, which is not only books, but also archive and museum objects such as photographs and jewellery. Because it would not fit inside the prescribed classifications, which were designed for more traditional (and overwhelmingly male-produced) historical library items, these artefacts of women's history would have been lost had a campaign not kept the collection whole.[46] However, it raises the point that while the Fawcett Library's collection represents a large (although, of course, not comprehensive) part of English women's history which can be researched and viewed in one place, there is no comparative single collection of Scottish women's and suffrage history. The items and literature of the Scottish suffrage campaigners are scattered around universities, museums and libraries, and not necessarily in Scotland, as is the case with Stephen's memoir, which is in Manchester's Working Class Movement Library. With the "already-there", as Withers defines it, of Scottish suffrage history fragmented, it is perhaps difficult for those who are interested to locate the information they desire.[47] This, then, gives the impression that there was no Scottish contingent of the suffrage movement, or that it was lesser than its English counterpart, with no structure or cohesion, which keeps Thomson and Stephen from getting the recognition they deserve for the record of their lives and political activism.

It is clear, then, that the focus on women's political histories of the metropolitan elite has excluded many significant voices, be those elderly, regional, socialist, working class or indeed many more that have not yet been explored at all. Stephen stated in *Spare Rib* in the 1970s that she believed books on suffrage histories were lacking in their portrayal of the diversity of the women's suffrage movement, and sadly this has not been fully rectified, even now as we enter the centenary of women achieving limited suffrage. Thankfully, languishing unpublished in archives, catalogued incorrectly due to a restrictive categorizing system and unfindable in online searches, are the stories which address these omissions. Jessie Stephen's "Submission Is for Slaves" and Elizabeth Thomson's "The Life Story of Miss Elizabeth Thomson" are surely just the beginning.

Notes

1. Leah Leneman, *A Guid Cause: The Women's Suffrage Movement in Scotland* (Edinburgh: Mercat, 1995), p. 1.
2. Leah Leneman, *The Scottish Suffragettes* (Edinburgh: NMS, 2000), p. 7.
3. Hilda Kean, "Some Problems of Constructing and Reconstructing a Suffragette"s Life: Mary Richardson, Suffragette, Socialist and Fascist", *Women's History Review*, 7.4 (1998): 475–93 (475).
4. Maroula Joannou, "'She Who Would Be Politically Free Herself Must Strike the Blow': Suffragette Autobiography and Suffragette Militancy", *The Uses of Autobiography*, ed. Julia Swindells (London: Taylor and Francis, 1995), pp. 31–44 (33).
5. Hilda Kean, "Public History and Popular Memory: Issues in Commemoration of the British Militant Suffrage Campaign", *Women's History Review*, 14.3–4 (2005): 581–602 (582).
6. June Purvis and Maureen Wright, "Writing Suffragette History: The Contending Autobiographical Narratives of the Pankhursts", *Women's History Review*, 14.3–4 (2005): 405–34 (426).
7. Krista Cowman, "A Footnote in History? Mary Gawthorpe, Sylvia Pankhurst, the Suffragette Movement and the Writing of Suffragette History", *Women's History Review*, 14.3–4 (2005): 447–66 (458–59).

8. Laura E. Nym Mayhall, "Creating the 'Suffragette Spirit': British Feminism and the Historical Imagination", *Women's History Review*, 4.3 (2006): 319–44 (321).
9. Elizabeth Thomson, "The Life Story of Miss Elizabeth Thomson, 1847–1918", GB 248 UGC 053, U of Glasgow Archive Services, *c.*1914. All biographical information is from this text, unless otherwise stated.
10. Jessie Stephen, "Submission Is for Slaves", PP/BIOG/16, Working Class Movement Lib., n.d. All biographical information is from this text, unless otherwise stated.
11. Gloden Dallas, "Jessie", *Spare Rib*, 32 (1975): 10–13 (11).
12. Thomson, p. 23.
13. Thomson, p. 16.
14. Thomson, p. 103.
15. Thomson, p. 106.
16. Thomson, p. 108.
17. Thomson, p. 31.
18. "Criminal Case File: Arabella Charlotte Scott, Edith Hudson, Elizabeth Thomson, Agnes Colquhoun Thomson (Suffragettes)", GB 234 HH16/44, National Records of Scotland, 1913–14.
19. "1918 Thomson, Elizabeth", Wills and Testaments Regiment, SC70/1/612, National Records of Scotland, 1918, p. 424.
20. Leneman, *Guid Cause*, p. 140.
21. Elizabeth Crawford, *The Women's Suffrage Movement in Britain and Ireland: A Regional Survey* (London: Routledge, 2006), p. 237.
22. June Hannam and Karen Hunt, *Socialist Women: Britain, 1880s to 1920s* (London: Routledge, 2001), pp. 105, 121
23. Stephen, p. 1.
24. Stephen, p. 8.
25. Stephen, p. 48.
26. Crawford, *Regional Survey*, p. 653.
27. Leneman, *Scottish Suffragettes*, p. 54.
28. Elspeth King, *The Scottish Women's Suffrage Movement* (Glasgow: People's Palace Museum, 1978), p. 24.
29. Stephen, pp. 48–49.
30. Stephen, p. 50.
31. Elizabeth Crawford, *The Women's Suffrage Movement: A Reference Guide 1866–1928* (London: Routledge, 2001), p. 524.
32. Barbara Winslow, *Sylvia Pankhurst: Sexual Politics and Political Activism* (London: UCL P, 1996), p. 66.
33. E. Sylvia Pankhurst, *The Suffragette Movement: An Intimate Account of Persons and Ideals* (London: Virago, 1988), p. 517.
34. Stephen, p. 70.
35. Jill Liddington and Jill Norris, *One Hand Tied Behind Us: The Rise of the Women's Suffrage Movement* (London: Rivers Oram, 2000), p. 224.
36. Leah Leneman, "A Truly National Movement", *The Women's Suffrage Movement: New Feminist Perspectives*, ed. Maroula Joannou and June Purvis (Manchester: Manchester UP, 1998), pp. 37–50 (47).
37. Stephen, p. 75.
38. Stephen, p. 77.
39. Stephen, p. 198.
40. Stephen, p. 122.

41. Kean, "Some Problems", 479.
42. Uri Margolin, "Telling Our Story: On 'We' Literary Narratives", *Language and Literature*, 5.2 (1996): 115–33 (132).
43. Margolin, 132.
44. Deborah Withers, *Feminism, Digital Culture and the Politics of Transmission: Theory, Practice and Cultural Heritage* (London: Rowman, 2015), p. 6.
45. Withers, p. 2.
46. Withers, p. 3.
47. Deborah Withers uses her example of the restrictive nature of the Dewey decimal system to illustrate how archives do not necessarily do well to promote the "already-there" of women"s history. Problems I have encountered in archives have included documents on the National Union of Women's Suffrage Societies incorrectly categorized as "suffragette" items, and court records which are tagged with only the names of the more well-known activists involved in the criminal case.

Disclosure statement

No potential conflict of interest was reported by the author.

ORCID

Gemma Elliott http://orcid.org/0000-0002-5483-3177

WRITING SUFFRAGE IN EDWARDIAN NOTTINGHAM

Val Wood

ABSTRACT
This article focuses on the provincial aspects of the Edwardian women's suffrage campaign in Nottingham, a city in the East Midlands, UK. The article explores writing about suffrage life in a range of formats—biography, journals, letters and archived materials, including notes of speeches—in respect of local activists—the suffragette Helen Watts, the Women's Social and Political Union organizer in Nottingham, Nellie Crocker and the suffragists Alice and Helena Dowson. Three distinctive pieces of writing have been selected. These include the speeches of Helen Watts; the diaries of Alice Dowson related by her granddaughter, Alix Meynell, which are presented as a biography entitled *What Grandmother Said* (1998); and the autobiographical writings of Nellie Crocker, entitled "Incidents in the Women's Suffrage Campaign", which she submitted to Girton College, Cambridge, in 1949. This personal testimony is important not only to aid understanding of the extent of the campaign for the vote in Nottingham, previously undocumented, but also for highlighting the interconnections between the protagonists under discussion and the wider suffrage movement during the period 1907–12.

Women suffrage supporters in Nottingham aligned themselves to two main female suffrage societies: the National Union of Women's Suffrage Societies (NUWSS) and the Women's Social and Political Union (WSPU). After 1908, many women actively supported the Church League for Women's Suffrage when a branch was established in the city. In 1909, anti-suffrage groups were also active and, for a brief period from 1917, there was a branch of the Women's Freedom League.[1] The Nottingham Women's Suffrage Society was established in 1881 and affiliated to the NUWSS in 1898. As in many other cities, family connections were important for developing and sustaining suffrage activism. The leader of the NUWSS in the city was Helena Dowson (née Brownsword). Helena's mother-in-law, Alice Dowson, had been the secretary of the Nottingham Suffrage Society from the 1880s until 1895, when the role transferred to Helena who, with her sisters-in-law Maud, Hilda and Lina, became the key personnel of the NUWSS in Nottingham.[2] Helena Dowson was born in 1866 into a Unitarian family aligned to the Liberal Party in Nottingham. In 1894, she married William Enfield Dowson, whose large family were, according to Meynell, clannish, non-conformist Unitarians, suffragists and steeped in provincial liberalism.[3] In 1898, Helena Dowson joined the executive committee of the NUWSS.[4] The core of the Nottingham society was Liberal women activists, many of whom were engaged in philanthropic work. They formed what Linda Walker notes as an "interlocking network of suffragist activists, bound by ties of kin, friendship and family".[5] Their philanthropy focused on the Nottingham Social Guild, the temperance movement and opposition to the prostitution of women. Many were also involved in the National Union of Women Workers, an umbrella group that brought together women's organizations engaged in voluntary social work, a branch of which had been established in the city in 1895.

The WSPU established a branch in Nottingham in 1906, as evidenced by a letter to the local Trade Union Council asking for help in its campaign to secure votes for women.[6] It is likely that the branch was led initially by Dorothy Pethick, who was employed as a superintendent of a girls' club in Nottingham and who was the sister of Emmeline Pethick-Lawrence, one of the national leaders of the WSPU. Dorothy was supported by Nell Kenney until 1908, when Rachel Barrett was based in the city as the WSPU's paid organizer, with Dorothy relocating to Leicester. That same year, May Burgis, a Nottingham-based schoolteacher, undertook the role of branch secretary, suggesting that the WSPU's paid organizers had had some success in gaining support in the city.[7] Helen Watts, for example, joined the branch in 1907 after she had heard Christabel Pankhurst speak in Nottingham in 1907.[8] In 1909, Ellen (Nellie) Crocker, a cousin of Emmeline Pethick-Lawrence, replaced Rachel Barrett as organizer in Nottingham, with Gladys Roberts from Leeds as her assistant.[9]

The Liberal Party's success in the 1906 general election resulted in Nottingham returning three Liberal Members of Parliament and galvanized the local NUWSS into greater activity. It held meetings, ran suffrage market stalls, organized fundraising concerts, held garden parties and staffed a suffrage shop. The WSPU also began to make its presence felt. In 1907, the local branch held a large meeting in the city, which was addressed by Christabel Pankhurst and Emmeline Pethick-Lawrence as part of a national campaign aimed at convincing provincial women to participate in the WSPU. In addition, it sought to persuade local Women's Liberal Associations to adopt the policy of withdrawing all help for Liberal candidates until the government introduced a sponsored bill to support women's suffrage. The WSPU meeting proved to be particularly volatile and noisy, and was disrupted by young men. Christabel Pankhurst, undaunted by the disruptions, declared that "the women of Nottingham are with us, and we shall come again shortly, we shall continue our tactics".[10] In December 1907, the Nottingham WSPU attempted to break up a meeting where Herbert Asquith, a Liberal Member of Parliament and the prime minister, was speaking, resulting in a number of suffragettes being ejected. In the spring of 1908, Emmeline Pankhurst spoke for the first time in the city, returning later to address a large outdoor demonstration which attracted a crowd that the local press estimated was up to 15,000 people, with the suffragettes recording attendances nearer to 30,000.[11] This demonstration had been preceded in June of that year by an outdoor demonstration organized by the Nottingham NUWSS with other groups in the East Midlands, which attracted smaller crowds of approximately 3000.[12] The difference between the two proceedings was immediately apparent. The NUWSS demonstration passed without incident, with its speaker, Mrs Stanbury, advocating a peaceful and constitutional demand for "what was fair and right", claiming that it was a "just and common-sense movement". The meeting concluded with a vote on the resolution "That this great meeting demands the vote for women on the same terms as it is, or may be given to men", and by the singing of the national anthem.[13] By contrast, the WSPU speakers at their demonstration, who had been met by noise and frequent interruptions, while also demanding the granting of the franchise to women on the same terms as men, claimed that presenting petitions and "Parliamentary pirouetting" had failed to bring women the vote and therefore the only alternative was to enter on a militant agenda.[14] They referred to the events in London of 30 June 1908 when a large deputation of suffragettes had gathered in Parliament Square to be met by a strong contingent of police officers, and there were many reports of assault and intimidation of the women supporters.

The events in Nottingham from the general election in 1906 through to 1908 provide a useful starting point for an analysis of the three pieces of suffrage writing identified in the introduction. Under consideration first are the diaries of the suffragist Alice Dowson, related in a biography by her granddaughter, Alix Meynell, published in 1998.[15] In the biography of her grandmother, Meynell dedicates one chapter to the subject of the women's suffrage campaign in Nottingham drawn from the diaries, a source which provides the most comprehensive contemporary account of the campaign in the city from the constitutional suffragist perspective. Although the reader has only extracts from the diaries, selected by Meynell, they do provide a wealth of personal reactions, including excitement, anger and disappointment, which are difficult to find in other sources. Alice Dowson (née Greg) was born in Cheshire in 1844 into a Unitarian family. She was married young, at the age of 19, to Ben Dowson, a lawyer, and they settled in Nottingham. Alice had a large family—10 children in total, eight boys and two girls, by the age of 34. Alice was involved from the 1860s with the campaign for the repeal of the Contagious Diseases Acts and she was also noted for her philanthropic work. She was secretary of the local branch of the Ladies' Committee for the Society for the Prevention of Cruelty to Children, the Nottingham Social Guild and an organization which she founded: the Lenton Visiting and Relief Society. Alice's support of anti-vivisection and concern for wider international matters, such as the atrocities committed against the Armenians in Turkey (1895) and the question of contagious diseases in India, reflects her engagement in multiple political and social causes during her life.[16] However, as Meynell relates, the women's suffrage cause occurs again and again in Alice's diaries from the 1870s onwards: "in a sense it was the background to all her political activity".[17]

The 1906 Liberal landslide election result was greeted by optimism in the Dowson family and should have set the stage for a government-sponsored bill. However, what followed was a series of disappointments when two further private member suffrage bills were talked out of Parliament in 1907. In her diary entry for March 1907, Alice related: "I had very black specs on and so disappointed that the Women's Suffrage Bill 'was talked' out again! We do feel angry—furious—with our craven MPs [Members of Parliament]".[18] Alice is also angered at the actions of the Liberal prime minister, Herbert Asquith, and she frequently alludes to his, in her words, "deceit" for failing to support a suffrage bill, and in a later entry calls him a "SNAKE".[19] Meynell draws the conclusion that it is this anger which results in Alice and the local branch of the NUWSS "doubling their efforts" during 1908, taking the suffrage campaign into the public sphere away from "drawing room meetings" and adopting tactics deployed by the leadership of the WSPU.

Local suffrage histories, often based on individual stories and personal writings, have been important in questioning conventional narratives about the hard and fast divisions between suffrage groups and in suggesting more complex personal views and alliances.[20] As Sandra Stanley Holton suggests: "the turn to personal history has made possible the construction of fresh narratives of the suffrage movement".[21] Meynell's biography, and the diaries on which it is based, certainly provides fresh insights. In addition to highlighting their growing disillusionment with the Liberal government, Meynell shows how this led the Dowson family to an increased sympathy with the WSPU. For example, she notes that Alice and Maud are invited to, and attend, a WSPU meeting at the Albert Hall in London at the personal invitation of Emmeline Pankhurst, to welcome suffragettes released from prison for acts of civil disobedience early in 1908. Alice records in her diary that this meeting was "very interesting & inspiring, they [the WSPU] collected over £5,000 !!! and Mrs Pankhurst and the other released prisoners were present; the speaking was good".[22] Then, in April 1908, when further suffrage meetings take place in Nottingham organized by the WSPU, Alice relates that at one addressed by Christabel Pankhurst she had "5 sons & 4 daughters there". In May that same year, Alice reports that Maud went to Nottingham for an evening meeting addressed by Mrs Pankhurst. When reports appeared in the local papers of the forcible feeding of suffragettes in Birmingham and elsewhere, who had gone on hunger strike in prison, Alice is swift to condemn the act, as this diary entry of September 1909 reflects: "Our blood was set on fire this morning on seeing in the papers that the suffragettes in prison are being forcibly fed! Words will not express our bitter indignation".[23] This sense of indignation is captured in the letter her daughter, Maud Dowson, sends to the local newspapers at Alice's bequest, stating "that women who in no sense can be called criminal [...] should be seised upon by men [...] gagged and made to submit to what amounts as torture" is unacceptable. She concludes by saying that whatever we may think of the methods of warfare, "surely we have by this time evolved some ordinary human sense of compassion".[24] There is a general sense in Meynell's account that the Dowson women believe the actions of the WSPU are justified in the light of the failure of successive private members bills to achieve assent and the intransigence of the prime minister, Herbert Asquith, even if they remain solidly, in Alice's words, "non-party & non militant".[25] Civil disobedience, after all, was a concept which Alice and her family were familiar with, and Alice had previously been active in organizing public protest in opposition to the Contagious Diseases Acts. Actions which included lobbying and attending political meetings with the purpose of intervening to ensure the issue was raised were seen as no different to those which the suffragettes were currently deploying. That violence should be enacted on women because of undertaking political action clearly rankled with Alice, and she believed that this violence was likely to lead to further violence against women, whichever strategy was deployed.

Anti-suffragist and anti-militant feelings were expressed by the Nottingham Women's Liberal Association and by the local branch of the National Union of Women Workers. Alice and Helena had helped to establish these groups and were leading figures within them, and Alice's diaries record the personal difficulties women experienced in facing criticism from old friends and colleagues. In 1908, women from the Liberal Association formed themselves into the Women's National Anti-Suffrage League and held several meetings in the city, to which Alice objected strongly.[26] Meynell references diary entries that hint at antagonism towards Alice from women within these organizations and her objection to the anti-suffrage elements within the local Liberal Party. This antagonism towards Alice may well have stemmed from the arrest of the local WSPU activist Helen Watts in London in February 1909. When Watts returned to Nottingham from her imprisonment in Holloway gaol, she was greeted, according to the local press, by a crowd of 50 WSPU and NUWSS activists. They hailed her with enthusiasm "to receive laurels from her sisters of the Lace City".[27] Some Liberal suffragists with more conservative views started to express their disquiet not only at the close relationships between the two main suffrage groups, but also at the support shown to the WSPU by prominent suffrage leaders in the city. Condemnation for the imprisonment of suffragettes was evident at two meetings hosted by the WSPU in the period immediately before Watts was arrested and after her release. In January 1909, at a large meeting where the regional WSPU organizer, Gladice Keevil, was the main speaker, the chair was taken by the Reverend J. M. Lloyd Thomas from the local Church League for Women's Suffrage. He expressed his satisfaction at the appearance of the Anti-Suffrage League, since any sort of opposition was "of value to a movement so full of vigour and vitality as the Women's Social and Political Union". In condemning the action of the government in imprisoning women who have demanded political liberty, the City Coroner and Liberal Mr C. L. Rothera noted that while the tactics of the suffragettes might be open to criticism, "let Nottingham women see to it that they were not backward in following the example of their leaders who had risked so much".[28] Similar sentiments were raised at the second meeting in March 1909, which was addressed by Emmeline Pankhurst. Buoyed up by the success of the meetings in Nottingham, she announced that the city needed a full-time organizer and, later that year, Nellie Crocker was appointed.[29]

When, from 1909 onwards, the NUWSS at the national level started to distance itself from the militancy of the WSPU, Helena Dowson felt compelled to write to Millicent Fawcett regarding her concerns about the working relationship between the suffrage groups in the city. In her letter, she states that: "we could not carry on the society in Nottingham without the people who would resign over a too strong condemnation of the WSPU".[30] Helena was concerned that there would be a disintegration of the country societies and she argued that militant sympathies were not always a weakness to the cause. She related later at a public meeting "that they [the WSPU] gave health and even life to the campaign […] showing their intense belief in their cause", and "the idea that non-militant suffragists should cease endeavouring to obtain the vote by constitutional methods until the militant women have forsaken their intended tactics was absurd".[31] In the letter to Fawcett, Helena reveals that two of her executive had only recently left the militant organization, and her belief on this evidence was that many women were in the "process of transition to constitutional methods", having first been brought into the movement by militancy. Is it wise to hurry them too much, she says, and for "something which is not of vital importance", adding that they give their work and money to the NUWSS and "before long I feel sure they will leave the S&PU al-together".

Throughout 1910, there were numerous meetings in Nottingham when both suffragette and suffragist activists came together.[32] The association between the groups related here is revealing, as more traditional histories of the movement tend to present an either–or situation in which an activist was either a law-abiding suffragist or a militant suffragette.[33] There is little evidence of any complete divide between the NUWSS and the WSPU in

Nottingham by 1910, although the city had not yet borne witness to the escalation of militancy to include arson and other destruction of property.

Overall, what Meynell's biography illustrates is the extent to which provincial suffrage campaigns evidence a wider level of activity than previously acknowledged. Meynell is keen to stress the hard work and commitment to the cause by the suffragists in Nottingham. She includes multiple diary entries in which there are details of "crammed" meetings, suffrage market stalls, concerts to raise funds and the staffing of the suffrage shop. Alice Dowson's diary entries also highlight that apart from imprisonment, there was little to differentiate the treatment of activists in a provincial city. Several of her entries for 1909 and 1910 deal with the unpleasantness experienced by suffragists: the rowdy, sometimes rough, nature of the open-air meetings—at one of which Alice recalls that it "swiftly became unruly and ended in a disgraceful riot"—and "the unpleasantness, the unfriendly, rude, populace and police" at the polling stations.[34] When the Women's Franchise (Conciliation Bill) faltered at the second reading in November 1910 and the events of Black Friday became known to Alice, she wrote:

> It was a critical day for suffragists at Westminster: this government continues to play with them [...] I was furious to hear how Mr Asquith has again disappointed us with his false and empty promises! and the Militants made a great riot in Westminster. Quite justified I think.[35]

It is interesting, however, that Alice never makes a direct reference to the WSPU or names the activists in Nottingham. In many respects, there is a separation in Alice's mind between the events that are taking place locally and those that occur in London. One of her last entries, dated 1911, expresses a degree of resignation regarding the suffrage campaign: "Mr Asquith and the Liberals remain in power, but the Irish hold the balance. Suffrage I fear stands a poor chance".[36]

Helen Watts' speeches provide further insights into the complexities of local suffrage activism. When historians use personal testimony, they tend to focus on diaries, letters and autobiographical writings, but speeches can also reveal a great deal about personal motivation, aims and ideas. The content, of course, is also affected by the audience to whom the speech is given. In contrast to Alice Dowson's diaries, the speeches of Helen Watts are confined to the period from March to November 1909. Watts was arrested outside the House of Commons in February 1909 for causing wilful obstruction, and then again in Leicester in September 1909. In the period from May to November 1909, she undertook several speaking engagements, which raised her profile as an accomplished orator and supporter of militancy.[37] There are eight speeches in total, seven typed and one handwritten; the latter is undated and may possibly relate to a later time.[38] Unlike the

Dowson family, Watts had no previous history of activism and joined the WSPU in 1907.

Helen Kirkpatrick Watts was born at Bishopswearmouth, County Durham, in July 1881, the eldest child of the Reverend Alan Hunter Watts and his wife, Ethelinda Woodrow Cassels. In 1893, the family relocated to Nottingham when Alan Watts took up the position as vicar of Holy Trinity Church, Lenton.[39] Little is known about Helen's life prior to her joining the WSPU in 1907 when she was already in her twenties. It appears that, as the eldest daughter, she was involved in the care of her younger siblings and the wider congregation of her father's parish. Watts' conversion to militancy begins after a year of what she refers to as "half-hearted support of our [WSPU] ideals and principles".[40] She is offered the opportunity to be part of a deputation to Parliament, which leads to her arrest and imprisonment in Holloway. Letters asking activists to participate came directly from Mrs Pankhurst, with the intention that the individual made her own arrangements without reference to the local branch.[41] Watts refers to this aspect in her address to local WSPU members at the welcome-back supper held at Morley's Café in March 1909, after her release from Holloway. She thanks members for having sent her to London and, when they express surprise, since they had known nothing until she had left, she relates that: "it was your unconscious influence, your earnestness and enthusiasm, that made me go [...] I would have been a poor little coward I am afraid, going just by myself".[42] Watts was, in fact, supported by two individuals, whom she openly acknowledges: Nell Kenney, who had been the WSPU organizer in the city and was in all probability the person who had nominated Watts' participation, and Kay Burgis, the secretary of the local branch. Watts referred to Kenney as an inspiration, "a real spiritual force in this town", and to Burgis as her intimate friend, who had been a tower of strength, providing her with the courage to participate. Watts provides an insight into the apprehension and anxiety which must have been felt by many women embarking on militant activities in the suffrage campaign, and the need to rationalize her actions. This first speech is personal, as it is made in private, with her family, friends and fellow activists in the local WSPU branch present, and therefore differs from the speeches she later made to more overtly public gatherings.

Watts is clearly aware that she will be required to go on speaking tours about her experiences. Her first speech was written with great care and attention to detail, and then revised, as two versions exist. Watts notes, for example, that the thought (a year ago) that she would go to prison would have "seemed to me an utterly impossible and absurd idea". She believed that she had lost a sense of herself and felt "that I was in a way the Nottingham Union". Using a literary reference, she claims that she "felt like the village maiden of Tennyson's poem, who found herself wedded to the Lord of Burleigh and who was perplexed night and morn with the burden of an honour unto which she was not born".[43] This is but one example of the use of literary references in her speeches where she frequently alludes to the ideals of honour for herself and later the honour of the suffrage cause. The experience of prison made a significant impression on Watts and formed the basis of later content in her speeches. It also provided her with a shared experience with a wider network of activists. Any misconceptions around her adoption of militant tactics had been swept aside as

> [...] she had learned and unlearnt a good deal [...] one blamed and ridiculed just as everyone else of the shrieking sisterhood [the suffragettes] she confessed [...] then the rightness and justice of the claim began to dawn, her conversion to militancy was complete.

Edwards has suggested that Watts' speech reflects the views of the Nottingham WSPU about the necessity of militant tactics and how these are justifiable.[44] Watts stresses, for example, that the deputations to Parliament which led to arrests should be viewed as socially acceptable tactics, as "it is one of the most recognised and constitutional methods of making grievances and is the special right as it should be of those who are unrepresentative of the governing body—the right of deputation and delegation".[45] At a public meeting in April 1909, Watts again reiterates this right to protest as a legitimate action, dismissing the talk that "goes on that this is the most unheard of, defiant and lawless proceeding". Invited to speak at an NUWSS meeting in the city about her experiences of prison, Watts informs them that when she came out of Holloway, she "was a double-dyed suffragette—purple, green and white all over"—and had been glad to wear the prison dress for the "sake of its splendid symbolism—it meant we were all women there". This special relationship of women together, shared only by those who have experienced imprisonment and, by implication, protest, is emphasized by Watts in her address to the local NUWSS branch. She follows this by stating that she now understands "a little better than before what the word comrade might mean".[46] In a rousing speech at Eastwood on 13 May 1909, Watts informs the meeting that the "suffragettes have come out of the drawing room, the study and the debating hall to appeal to the new sovereign power in the country the people". Her implication here is that the non-militant NUWSS needed to adopt militant tactics.

When hunger strikes, first used by Marion Dunlop in July 1909 as a protest against the refusal to classify suffragettes as political prisoners, were adopted by the WSPU more generally, Watts justified this course of action as morally defensible because of its results. In September 1909, Watts was arrested in Leicester on a charge of disorderly conduct for attempting to enter a building where Winston Churchill was speaking. She adopted the tactic of a hunger strike and was released after five days. Watts' experience of her time in prison in Leicester strengthened her resolve and marked a change in her political views, as evident in her talk at Morley's Café in Nottingham after her release.[47] Her typed speech is, as previously, clearly structured and blends the personal with the political. It provides a comprehensive account of her treatment and time in prison, including the use of hunger striking. Watts reflects on how the whole tone of the Leicester prison was very different to that of Holloway, but she still experienced considerable disquiet, noting that: "nearly all the time I was in prison I was dreading some sudden attempt on the part of the officials to compel us, by using violence to wear the prison dress or to break our fast". Nonetheless, she argues that "personal fears and feelings do not matter [...] the one thing that will matter is have we kept straight on". This was the first time that Watts had adopted the hunger strike and, although she was threatened with forcible feeding, this was not carried out. Again, she seeks to justify these new tactics by stating that although it was "a desperate line to take up it had completely justified itself by results, for self-sacrifice could only convince any woman or human of the morally defensible intentions of the action".[48] Watts is careful to blend the personal self-sacrifice of the suffragettes with political activism, and employs similar battlefield symbols to those used by Christabel Pankhurst. She writes that just as a soldier on the battlefield feels that, "at whatever cost to himself, his country's flag must be kept flying, so we felt that, for the honour of our cause [...] we MUST protest".[49] She concludes that they are fighting for a human right, on absolutely simple and straightforward principles. In April 1909, Watts was awarded the Holloway Prison Medal at the Albert Hall in London—the first time that medals had been awarded to suffragettes who had been imprisoned. Later, she received the Hunger Strike Medal.[50]

Although prison and the adoption of militant actions do form the main component of her speeches, Watts still outlines wider concerns about the role of women in society. Speaking at Eastwood in May 1909, she informs the audience that it is only through achieving the vote that women will be able to combat the "sweating evil, intemperance, bad housing and many other miserable conditions in England today". Later in the same year, at Midsomer Norton, Somerset, Watts reiterates that it is through the vote that women will become citizens and that there will be improvements to the intolerable conditions that women faced.[51] These later speeches that encompass issues of social justice suggest a change in Watts' views, but November was her last public-speaking engagement. Watts left Nottingham sometime in 1910. Her last recorded action was a protest outside a meeting when she was arrested, but the case against her was dismissed. Interestingly, she did not participate in the census protest of April 1911. Instead, as Rowena Edlin-White notes, she was a boarder in the same house as her brother Neville, a schoolmaster, in Chilcompton, near Bath, and she complied with the census.[52]

The last piece of suffrage writing to be considered is the autobiographical manuscript of the suffragette activist Nellie Crocker, who had lived in Nottingham since July 1909. Crocker, the daughter of a doctor, was born in 1872 in Stogumber, Somerset, and was the cousin of Dorothy Pethick and her older sister, Emmeline Pethick-Lawrence. She joined the WSPU in the autumn of 1907 after her resignation from the post of honorary secretary of the Women's Liberal Association in Wellington in protest at the Liberal government's lack of support for women's enfranchisement.[53] It is possible that before her involvement in politics, Crocker had worked for a girls' club, and it is noted in an early newspaper report that Nellie, with her sister Emma, had been successful in University Extension Lectures.[54] Prior to residing in Nottingham, Crocker had been the WSPU organizer for Yorkshire, based in Sheffield. She was one of the principal speakers on the platform at the WSPU's June 1908 Hyde Park demonstration and, in June 1909, was arrested and imprisoned as part of the WSPU deputation to the House of Commons. Appointed as the new WSPU organizer for Nottingham, she arrived immediately after her release from Holloway following a hunger strike. Crocker was a skilled and experienced organizer who established herself quickly in the city, opening a suffragette shop and providing leadership for the branch. She organized several WSPU meetings in the city during 1910 at the time of the general election of that year, including a joint meeting with the local NUWSS, when Lady Constance Lytton spoke about her experiences of imprisonment. Helen Watts and Helena Dowson were in the audience. In November 1910, when the progress of the Women's Franchise Conciliation Bill faltered and then stalled completely, the NUWSS and the WSPU joined forces in protest in a large London demonstration which became known as Black Friday. Included in the number of arrests that day were Nellie Crocker and three other members of the Nottingham WSPU. In April 1911, Crocker participated in the census protest in Nottingham and then joined a significant contingent of women from both suffrage groups in the city in the Women's Coronation Procession in London in June 1911, having previously been in Newton Abbot for the mid-Devon by-election with Dorothy Pethick. In 1912, Crocker was arrested again in London for damaging property and, while in prison awaiting sentencing, wrote to Helen Watts, who was now training as a nurse at the Royal National Hospital for Rheumatic Diseases in Bath. This letter is included amongst the copies of Watts' speeches in the Nottinghamshire archives. In her letter to Watts, Crocker relates that she is having a much worse time than those who had been convicted and "never did my soul so long to be found guilty".[55] Crocker was released in June 1912 and returned to Nottingham where a by-election was being contested in Ilkeston, in nearby Derbyshire. However, by mid November 1912, Crocker had left both Nottingham and the WSPU and returned to Somerset.

In 1949, at the age of over 70, Crocker presented a seven-page autobiographical manuscript to Girton College, Cambridge, entitled "Incidents in the Women's Suffrage Campaign".[56] Crocker claimed in the manuscript that "there was talk years ago of my going to your University [Girton College] but it did not mature", and this may well have been her motive in lodging the manuscript there. In her introductory letter to the college librarian, she states that she hopes that the contents will be useful, noting: "Modern Young Women seem unaware of the price paid for their political and social emancipation and modern historians have greatly ignored the struggle".[57] In her manuscript, Crocker references two autobiographies: that of her cousin, Emmeline Pethick-Lawrence, entitled *My Part in a Changing World* (1938), and Constance Lytton's 1914 account of her time in prison.[58] In doing so, she indicates the importance of family ties and also, in Constance Lytton's case, implies that prison experiences are important. Much has been written about the importance of suffrage autobiographies in shaping our views of the movement and the nature of militancy.[59] It is important, therefore, to go beyond the most well-known texts in order to encompass a wide range of experiences—in particular, given the diverse ways in which they were written. The title of Crocker's script in many ways reflects the content of her autobiography as it comprises a set of incidents or stories in the suffrage campaign, covering the period 1909–12, with no reference to specific dates or recorded historical events. Crocker's writing is descriptive and pragmatic in approach, giving little sense of what happened in a coherent way. Common themes do emerge: there is reference to arrest and imprisonment, the deputations to Parliament, speaking at open-air meetings and organizing interventions at by-elections. She notes, for example, that although she has been frequently arrested in the city (there is no direct reference to this actually being Nottingham), because she was well known, she was always released without charge, adding: "nothing adds more to our cause than rough treatment and imprisonment". As this quotation indicates, Crocker placed her individual actions within a collective story, which was common within suffrage autobiographies.[60]

The narrative she presents appears to be fresh in her mind, even though it occurred nearly 40 years earlier. She recalls, for example, that the deputations to Parliament were met with great hustling and violence, and how Mrs Leigh, an enthusiastic speaker, had purposely learnt ju-jitsu. According to Crocker, she had practised this so cleverly that it once took six policemen to arrest her. There is also a reference to Emily Davison, whom she had known and been imprisoned with, but no other fellow activists are referred to in the manuscript. For example, her co-worker Gladys Roberts is never named in her script, and her reasons for this are not clear.

Crocker's skills lay very much with organizing and interventions on behalf of the WSPU in by-elections. We know, for example, that she was the WSPU organizer present at seven by-elections across England and at the Scottish Montrose Burghs in 1908.[61] Her manuscript does relate the detail of a specific by-election in 1910 at Retford in north Nottinghamshire, approximately 20 miles from her lodgings in Nottingham. Crocker hired a car and engaged a driver, informing the reader that: "our good driver armed himself with a large iron rod which he placed under his seat to protect himself". She then goes on to relate an incident at an open-air meeting that turned into a hostile gathering, which, she declares, had been orchestrated by the Liberals. Crocker and Gladys Roberts were rescued by the host of the local hotel, who was, in her words, "[a] conservative—favourable as their cry had been Keep the Liberal candidates out". Having failed to hold a meeting outside, she hired a hall—the local theatre—and the meeting proceeded without further trouble. What is interesting is the reflection that follows the account, in which Crocker admits to apprehension prior to meetings, particularly when the territory was new: "There was at that time, always these risks to face in a new constituency and softly be it spoken sometimes the Wild Women of Westminster as the suffragettes had been dubbed, they had the largest audiences of either party".

There is a great deal of humour and sardonic comment in Crocker's accounts. She relates, for example, how she found two books in her prison cell. One was the Bible, open at the story of the young man at Dotham,[62] and the other was entitled *A Happy Home and How to Keep It*, in which the first sentence she reads is a "Vitiated atmosphere spells death"—a good augury, she notes, for their movement as a whole. Other incidences include the outline of a story which has been variously recorded regarding the fountain at Long Eaton, a village on the Nottingham border. Crocker records that the "roughs came, lifted up the street gratings of the Market Place, threw the indescribable slush they secured at the speaker [Crocker] hoping she would go away". There is also a humorous account of her co-worker being hustled out of a political meeting, the steward falling and her friend falling on top of him.

Crocker's manuscript provides a different perspective to what we know about the familiar characteristics of suffragettes. It is often noted that many suffrage activists were vegetarians. Crocker, however, tells an amusing story of a suffragette who was a meat eater. Crocker had been "charged with her comfort" during and after imprisonment, but the suffragette was so collapsed that she was sent to a nursing home to recuperate, where only vegetarian food was served. Addressing a meeting together a few days later, they were greeted by a local doctor's wife, who invited them to stay. When she enquired what the suffragette who had been imprisoned would like for dinner, Crocker notes: "A bloody beef steak she said and sure enough it was put before her". Crocker diffuses the situations she finds herself in through humour and anecdote, and is always self-deprecating in her accounts. Krista Cowman suggests that suffragettes often used humour not only to alleviate some of the stresses of political campaigning, but also to counterbalance the over-formal and male-dominated Edwardian politics.[63] As these extracts demonstrate, Crocker was certainly skilled in the use of put-downs and wit.

Crocker's account also provides material to add to our understanding of the experience of imprisonment. She spent significant periods of time in prison, where she undertook two hunger strikes. While there, she challenged the conditions under which she was held and demanded the right to be recognized as a political prisoner. In one account, Crocker notes that the prison governor visited her cell with his hat on, "as if he was going to the stables". She upbraids him for his lack of politeness to her and notes that, for the remaining six weeks of her prison term, he always left his hat on the chair at the entrance. She also refused to accept the financial payment of twopence presented to her as she left prison, as this identified her as an ordinary prisoner. Returning from Holloway prison, she reflects that she had greatly benefited from the succession of suffragette prisoners who had served varied sentences, noting that "the first batch of them had a hectic time". It is possible to view Crocker as a formidable personality and an individual prepared to challenge authority despite the personal cost. In her writing, she commented that such "sacrifice is deemed of small account in comparison to emancipation". When her case was finally heard after her arrest in 1912 in London for window-breaking, she gave her reasons for doing so "as a protest against the way women have been treated". This was a reference to the rough treatment of those women who tried to reach Parliament on Black Friday.

Little is known about Crocker after she left the WSPU. It is surmised that her departure was related to events surrounding her relatives, Emmeline and Frederick Pethick-Lawrence, key leaders and financial backers for the national organization, who had been ousted from the WSPU in 1912 after growing differences with Emmeline and Christabel Pankhurst. There is no specific evidence as to why Crocker left but, as Brian Harrison notes, the Pethick family were very close and potentially it was simply a case of choosing family over the party.[64] Crocker's replacement in Nottingham in 1912 was Charlotte Marshall, who had a long history of militancy and had been imprisoned many times. During her time in Nottingham, an increase in acts of militancy, including arson, was reported.[65] It is likely that Crocker herself was experiencing doubts regarding the direction of the WSPU and was apprehensive about the introduction of militancy in a city where she was well known and had spent four years campaigning with all the suffrage groups. She did, however, join the Suffragette Fellowship, which had been founded as the Suffragette Club by Edith How Martyn in 1926. The aims of the Fellowship were to perpetuate the memory of the pioneers and the outstanding events connected with them, especially in relation to the militant suffrage campaign.[66] Crocker made financial contributions and left the residue of her estate to the Fellowship. Helen Watts was also a member of the Suffragette Fellowship and attended the annual suffrage reunions.[67]

The suffrage writing selected for this article represents different perspectives and strategies of the campaign for the vote. The three protagonists are nonetheless linked by time, place and their individual participation in the movement in a provincial city. Alice's diaries provide a valuable everyday picture of the long campaign for women's suffrage, and highlight the contribution made to it by the constitutionalists. The Dowson family continued to be politically active after 1912, organizing and participating in the 1913 NUWSS pilgrimage and then, in 1914, helping to set up a branch of the Women Citizens Association in Nottingham. In 1919, Helena became one of the first women city councillors in Nottingham and vice-chair of the national executive of the Liberal Party. Despite the failure of the Liberal government to embrace fully women's suffrage, it is Helena's adherence to liberalism and the Liberal Party, rather than gender, that remained a constant throughout her political life. When the Representation of the People Act was passed in 1918, Alice Dowson, now elderly, simply notes that women's suffrage is "an accomplished fact! The result of so many years' labour".[68] Watts and Crocker were no longer politically active after 1911 and 1912, respectively, but remained committed to the Suffragette Fellowship. Watts has now become an inspiring local heroine and details are known about her life. Crocker, on the other hand, is less well known. Her autobiographical writings are in manuscript form and therefore not easily accessible, while she downplayed her own importance in what is often an impersonal account of the suffrage struggle. Nonetheless, her autobiography is rich in content and provides valuable insights into aspects of suffrage history. Collectively, the three pieces of suffrage writing discussed here demonstrate the extent and complexity of the suffrage campaign in one provincial city and contribute to new understandings of suffrage history from a local perspective. As the narrative of events suggests, there was, at times, greater activity in Nottingham than that witnessed in places of a similar size, and a close working relationship between the two main suffrage groups, which persisted despite the escalation of militancy. The personal writing selected provides us with a real sense of time and place, and an insight into what it must have felt like to be engaged in suffrage activism.

Notes

1. A reference is made to a branch of the Women's Freedom League being active in Nottingham in 1918 in Claire Eustance, "Daring to Be Free: The Evolution of Women's Political Identities in the Women's Freedom League 1907–1908", PhD thesis, U of York, 1993.
2. Dowson Papers, Nottinghamshire Archive Office, DD/523/4, Nottingham.

3. Dame Alix Meynell, *What Grandmother Said: The Life of Alice Dowson 1844–1927, Based on Her Diaries* (Cambridge: Colt, 1998).
4. Elizabeth Crawford, *The Women's Suffrage Movement: A Reference Guide 1866–1928* (London: Routledge, 2001), pp. 173–74.
5. Linda Walker, "Gender, Suffrage and Party: Liberal Women's Organisations", *Suffrage Outside Suffragism: Women's Vote in Britain, 1880–1914*, ed. Myriam Boussahba-Bravard (Houndmills: Palgrave, 2007), pp. 77–101 (78).
6. Peter Wyncoll, *The Nottingham Labour Movement, 1880–1939* (London: Lawrence, 1985), p. 95.
7. Actual membership has been hard to gauge for the WSPU in Nottingham. Whitmore, drawing from an analysis of the *Votes for Women* newspaper, suggests that there were 350 members in this period, but this has been difficult to substantiate. R. Whitmore, *Alice Hawkins and the Suffragette Movement in Edwardian Leicester* (Derby: Breedon, 2007), p. 172.
8. Rowena Edlin-White, *Helen Kirkpatrick Watts: Nottingham Suffragette 1881–1972* (Nottingham: Smallprint, 2016).
9. Crawford, *Reference Guide*, p. 35.
10. *Nottingham Evening Post*, 3 Dec. 1907.
11. *Votes for Women*, July 1908.
12. *Nottingham Guardian*, 12 June 1908.
13. *Nottingham Guardian*, 12 June 1908.
14. *Nottingham Daily Express*, 18 July 1908.
15. Meynell's biography was written when she was aged 95 and she herself had enjoyed a long and active public life as a senior civil servant, which she related in her autobiography, *Public Servant, Private Woman: An Autobiography* (London: Gollancz, 1988).
16. Meynell, p. 181.
17. Meynell, p. 240.
18. Meynell, p. 243.
19. Meynell, p. 244.
20. See, for example, Elizabeth Crawford, *The Women's Suffrage Movement in Britain and Ireland: A Regional Survey* (Abingdon: Routledge, 2006).
21. Sandra Stanley Holton, "Challenging Masculinities: Personal History and Micro History in Feminist Studies of the Women's Suffrage Movement", *Women's History Review*, 20.5 (2011): 829–41 (835).
22. Meynell, p. 244.
23. Meynell, p. 245.
24. Meynell, p. 245.
25. Meynell, p. 246.
26. Meynell, p. 241.
27. *Nottingham Evening News*, 20 Mar. 1909.
28. *Nottingham Evening News*, 25 Jan. 1909.
29. *Nottingham Evening News*, 27 Mar. 1909.
30. Helena B. Dowson toMillicent Fawcett, Oct.1909, Women's Suffrage Collection, Manchester Central Lib., Manchester.
31. *Nottingham Evening Post*, 26 June 1914.
32. On 26 July 1910, the *Nottingham Evening News* noted that there was a joint meeting between the Nottingham NUWSS, the WSPU and the Church League for Women's Suffrage, which argued that the fight for the vote by women was absolutely moral. A meeting addressed by Ethel Snowden was

attended by all the suffrage groups in the city, and NUWSS representatives supported a meeting addressed by Adela Pankhurst in the Market Place in July 1910.

33. Leah Leneman, "A Truly National Movement: The View from Outside London", *The Women's Suffrage Movement: New Feminist Perspectives*, ed. Maroula Joannou and June Purvis (Manchester: Manchester UP, 1998), pp. 37–50 (43).
34. Meynell, pp. 253–54.
35. Meynell, p. 254.
36. Meynell, p. 254.
37. Research undertaken by Rowena Edlin-White on Helen Watts, 2016.
38. The archive relating to Helen Watts can be found at the Nottinghamshire Archive Office (DD/893-6), where photocopies of her papers were deposited after their discovery in an unclaimed trunk at Avonmouth Docks in the early 1980s. The original archive contained 23 letters dated 1909–1914 to Helen or her family and 8 written speeches dated 1909.
39. There were seven younger siblings, including Alice Margaret (1882), who was also involved in the suffrage cause; Neville Hunter (1883), a schoolteacher; and Ethelinda Bertha (1886), a teacher.
40. Speech dated Mar. 1909.
41. Gemma Edwards, "Infectious Innovations? The Diffusion of Tactical Innovation in Social Movement Networks: The Case of Suffragette Militancy", *Social Movement Studies*, 13.1 (2014): 48–69.
42. Speech dated 18 May 1909, Birmingham; Nottinghamshire Archive Office, DD/993/4.
43. Speech dated Mar. 1909 at the welcome supper at Morley's Café, Nottingham, to the local WSPU branch after Watts' return from London and her first imprisonment; Nottinghamshire Archive Office, DD/893/4.
44. Edwards, 52.
45. Speech dated Mar. 1909.
46. Undated speech to the Nottingham NUWSS, 1909. The title states: "At a meeting in the Mikado café Nottingham of the NUWSS"; Nottinghamshire Archive Office, DD/893/4.
47. Speech dated 17 Sept. 1909. Watts addressed the local WSPU branch at Morley's Café after her release from Leicester prison; Nottinghamshire Archive Office, DD/893/4.
48. Speech dated 17 Sept. 1909.
49. Speech dated 17 Sept. 1909.
50. Edlin-White, p. 9.
51. Speech dated 27 Nov. 1909 at Midsomer Norton; Nottinghamshire Archive Office, DD/893/4.
52. Edlin-White, p. 10.
53. Crawford, *Reference Guide*, p. 153.
54. List supplied in the *Western Gazette Newspaper* (June 1892) and *Totnes Weekly Times* (May 1898), which reported that under the guidance of Miss N. Crocker the girls had been undertaking drill and recitation.
55. Letter from Nellie Crocker to Helen Watts, Mar. 1912; Nottinghamshire Archive Office, DD/896.

56. Comprising five pages of typescript without numbers, with a covering letter, the manuscript was deposited in Girton College, Cambridge, Library Archive 1949, by Nellie Crocker. Archive Reference GC/ RF8/1/4/1.
57. Letter from Nellie Crocker to the librarian at Girton College, 19 Jan. 1949.
58. Emmeline Pethick-Lawrence, *My Part in a Changing World* (London: Gollancz, 1938); Constance Lytton, *Prisons and Prisoners: The Stirring Testimony of a Suffragette* (1914; London: Virago, 1988).
59. See, for example, Hilda Kean, "Searching for the Past in Present Defeat: The Construction of Historical and Political Identity in British Feminism in the 1920s and 1930s", *Women's History Review*, 3.1 (1994): 57–80; Maroula Joannou, "She Who Would Be Politically Free Herself Must Strike the First Blow: Suffragette Autobiography and Suffragette Militancy", *The Uses of Autobiography*, ed. Julia Swindells (London: Taylor, 1995), pp. 31–44; Laura E. Nym Mayhall, "Creating the Suffragette Spirit: British Feminism and the Historical Imagination", *Women's History Review*, 4.3 (1995): 319–44.
60. June Purvis and Maureen Wright, "Writing Suffragette History: The Contending Autobiographical Narratives of the Pankhursts", *Women's History Review*, 14.3–4 (2005): 405–34 (407).
61. Crawford, *Reference Guide*, p. 153.
62. Biblical reference in the Old Testament, Book of Genesis, to a young man who has spent his days in a musty counting house and dreams of his release.
63. Krista Cowman, "Doing Something Silly: The Uses of Humour by the Women's Social and Political Union, 1903–1914", *International Review of Social History*, 52.S15 (2007): 259–74.
64. Brian Harrison, "Lawrence, Emmeline Pethick, Lady Pethick-Lawrence", *Oxford Dictionary of National Biography* (Oxford: Oxford UP, 2004), 16 Dec. 2016 https://doi.org/10.1093/ref:odnb/37846.
65. There was a recorded increase in militancy in Nottingham after 1912, including the burning down of the Nottingham Boat Club and the arrest of Eileen Casey when she was found with bomb-making equipment on the day of the visit by King George V and Queen Mary to Nottingham. Casey was tried in the city and sentenced to 15 months' imprisonment in Birmingham.
66. Crawford, *Reference Guide*, p. 661; Hilda Kean, "Public History and Popular Memory: Issues in the Commemoration of the British Militant Suffrage Campaign", *Women's History Review*, 14.3–4 (2005): 581–602.
67. Edlin-White, p. 9.
68. Meynell, p. 258.

Disclosure statement

No potential conflict of interest was reported by the author.

THE "SORDID STORY" OF AN UNWANTED CHILD: MILITANCY, MOTHERHOOD AND ABORTION IN ELIZABETH ROBINS' *VOTES FOR WOMEN!* AND *WAY STATIONS*

Emma Liggins

ABSTRACT
This article reconsiders representations of the militant suffragette in two texts by the radical writer Elizabeth Robins: *Votes for Women!* (1907) and her collection of political speeches and articles, *Way Stations* (1913). Her plea for twentieth-century women writers to create new roles for women outside those of wives and sweethearts can be read in relation to the creation of her "exceptional" suffragette heroine, who thrives on her singleness in her 1907 play. Focusing particularly on the taboo issues of abortion and unmarried motherhood, the author considers the ways in which Robins developed the fallen woman on stage narrative in the early twentieth century, and how childlessness is shown to be both necessary and problematic for the suffragette heroine. The author also reassesses Robins' complex commentaries on militancy and "quiet propaganda" in her suffrage speeches and pamphlets.

The meanings of militancy as a form of political protest have generated considerable discussion amongst suffrage historians and feminist critics. In 2000, Sandra Stanley Holton noted the gaps in our knowledge of the militant tactics adopted by different suffrage organizations.[1] Writing on the Women's Freedom League founded in 1907, Claire Eustance has explored the elasticity of the term, showing how it encompassed a spectrum of positions from rebellion and "non-violent resistance" to window-smashing and arson.[2] Women writers' responses to the suffrage campaign were always informed by an awareness of different forms of political protest, raising broader questions about class, family and femininity. In this article, I examine some of the diverse meanings of militancy in relation to abortion, childlessness and the differences between ordinary and "exceptional" women in the writing of the actress turned activist Elizabeth Robins, linking this to her involvement with the Women Writers' Suffrage League (WWSL), formed in 1908.

A reconsideration of Elizabeth Robins' political arguments about militancy and motherhood, in the context of shifting attitudes towards what it meant to be militant between 1907 and 1914, can illuminate the "sordid story" of a suffragette's lost child in her pioneering suffrage drama *Votes for Women!* (1907). Dramatizing the effects of an illegal abortion, which was subject to censorship in the early twentieth century, allowed Robins to expose stereotypes of the dowdy, childless suffragette as limited and limiting. The significance of "quiet propaganda" and the role of the "ordinary woman" in *Way Stations*, a collection of suffrage speeches and articles for the press published in 1913, are revealing of Robins' ongoing negotiation of the woman writer's special role in advancing the cause.

The Women Writers' Suffrage League

As president of the WWSL, a suffragist organization formed in 1908 which dedicated itself to achieving political change by "the use of the pen",[3] Elizabeth Robins became a trailblazer for a new kind of heroine. An American actress and novelist who had moved to London in 1888, Robins was primarily known to the British public for her leading roles in the radical drama of Henrik Ibsen, such as Hedda Gabler in 1891. She remained active in both theatrical and political circles, joining the Women's Social and Political Union (WSPU) in 1906 at the end of her acting career, and was admired by the Pankhursts for her suffrage speeches. In her lecture "The Women Writers" at the Criterion Theatre in 1910, included in *Way Stations*, she famously urged members of the newly formed League to produce alternative narratives for women outside of marriage and motherhood:

> Enough has not been made of such traces as history preserves of significant lives lived by women [...] Your Great Adventure is to report her faithfully. So that her children's children reading her story shall be lifted up—proud and full of hope. "Of such stuff", they shall say, "our mothers were! Sweethearts and wives—yes, and other things besides, leaders, discoverers, militants, fighting every form of wrong". (178, 181)

This has generally been read in relation to unearthing these "significant lives" which lie outside conventional notions of women's history, rather than in terms of what is suggested about the relationship between motherhood and militancy. In bequeathing their legacy to their grandchildren, the leaders, discoverers and militants must necessarily position themselves in relation to the next generation and the one after that, which involves a confrontation with their attitudes to reproduction. In Robins' writing of the early twentieth century, the suffrage heroine's militant characteristics had to be reconciled with her (lost) maternity.

According to her biographer Angela V. John, Robins, a "committed suffragette" and public persona in the Edwardian period, "took on the establishment both from without and from within, becoming an apologist for militancy in the daily press".[4] Her American identity set her apart from her contemporaries and, as both insider and outsider, she was perhaps well placed to offer an original insight into the British suffrage movement. Whilst her work for the theatre is more well known, *Way Stations*, often ignored by critics, has not been considered in relation to other feminist arguments of the suffrage era about motherhood and singleness. Robins was developing her views on the "exceptional" woman and the militant's embracing of publicity; these can be read alongside questionings of the maternal instinct and the campaign for birth control by other suffrage feminists such as Cicely Hamilton and Stella Browne, the campaigner for reproductive rights. Hamilton, also known as an actress and playwright, had formed the WWSL with Bessie Hatton and was connected with Robins through its sister organization, the Actresses' Franchise League (1908), dedicated to the staging of suffrage drama.[5]

The woman writer's special role in social reform and legacy for "the Women Writers of the future" (180) is paramount in a series of speeches later included in *Way Stations* delivered to the WWSL between 1908 and 1910. As Sowon S. Park has shown, WWSL writers believed that their work should be "Interventionist", aimed at the common reader but also "exploit [ing] its potential to bring about social change".[6] The leaflet outlining the function and scope of the society asserts its aim "that members will ensure ventilation of the subject [of the emancipation of women] in such ways as are open to them—by writing articles, taking part in newspaper correspondence, etc." (83), and lists key members, including Olive Schreiner, May Sinclair, Sarah Grand, Beatrice Harraden, Violet Hunt, Mrs Havelock Ellis and Evelyn Sharp. This "ventilation" is evident in her lecture "Suffrage Camp Revisited" of 1908, which argues that some women writers of the past have "borne false witness" to women's delight in the domestic. The conservative rhetoric of Sarah Ellis's conduct books in the 1840s is contrasted with Mrs Jamieson's progressive proclamations on woman's desired movement into her "real sphere" outside the home. The fact that Victorian women writers had not sufficiently been able to challenge notions of "what is called [woman's] proper sphere" (50) becomes a call to arms:

> What came of all this brave nineteenth-century talk that has to our ears such a twentieth-century ring? Why didn't these women accomplish more? Why have they left so much for you to do? [...] These excellent people failed to further the Cause they advocated, because they tried to do alone what can only be accomplished if we work together. (50)

This critique of the "exceptional" woman, who tries to go it alone, is coupled with the belief that by working together, "shoulder to shoulder" (53), twentieth-century women writers can inspire woman to move into her "real sphere". In a later speech, connections are made between Mary Wollstonecraft's arguments about women's desire for citizenship and Cicely Hamilton's *Marriage as a Trade* (1909), which exposes marriage as a form of prostitution. In the latter, Hamilton attacked "the ideal of the 'angel'" before criticizing women writers for creating "lop-sided" female characters, "creatures existing only for love and maternity", which leave readers "unconvinced, dissatisfied and even irritated".[7] Silly angels, like the conventional wives and sweethearts, would not take centre stage in suffrage writing. Although it did not directly discuss politics, Hamilton's play *Diana of Dobson's* (1908) allowed the woman writer to ventilate concerns about sweated labour through the speeches of an overworked shop girl who dared to stand up to her capitalist employer. Hamilton also pointed out in *Marriage as a Trade* that "the unwanted child—other than the illegitimate—has played practically no part in [women's literature]".[8] This suggests that she shared Robins' interest in representing the desire for childlessness, as well as addressing concerns about illegitimacy. Robins' urging of women writers "to correct the false ideas about women which many writers of the past have fostered" (85) could be interpreted in terms of asking the League to turn away from conventional notions of marriage and motherhood towards female friendship, militancy and strength through citizenship.

Votes for Women! and stereotypes of the suffragette

According to Naomi Paxton, suffrage drama flourished between 1908 and 1914. Plays written and produced by the Actresses' Franchise League, as "unapologetic propaganda pieces", enabled male and female playwrights to move beyond the limitations of the commercial theatre.[9] Yet propaganda should not be seen as a dirty word, as was sometimes the case in the modernist period; Katharine Cockin reminds us that "women's writing for the stage [...] has been subject to prejudiced judgements" which still need to be challenged by feminist critics.[10] As members of the Actresses' Franchise League, both Robins and Hamilton appropriated the aims of the WWSL for the stage, allowing outspoken and politically aware heroines to eclipse the role of the silly angel. Written in 1907, drawing on Robins' moment of conversion to the cause in Trafalgar Square in 1906, *Votes for Women!* was one of the first suffrage dramas, staged a few years before suffragette activities escalated into window-smashing and arson. In this new genre, the political woman's embracing of publicity was reflected in new theatrical settings such as the London streets and meeting halls; Robins' play was praised for its innovative use of a crowd scene of 48 actors set in Trafalgar Square, which mimicked a suffrage rally with all its heckling and interruptions.[11] Drawing-room discussions often captured women's excitement at entering public spaces and drew attention to this occupation of new territory; the opening address to the audience of Mrs Harlow Phibbs' comic monologue *The Mother's Meeting* (1913) is: "Bit surprised to see me, eh? You'll be more surprised when you hear where I've been".[12]

Comic stereotypes of both suffragists and anti-suffragists featured in many of these plays, as a means of drawing in the audience. In the first drawing-room scene of *Votes for Women!*, a range of characters discuss recent acts by the newly formed WSPU, such as the interruptions of parliamentary speeches and speaking in public about women's trade unions. Differentiating between the dreaded "political women" and "the charming wives and sweethearts who help to win seats", anti-suffragists, including the Liberal Member of Parliament St John Greatorex, dismiss as "nonsense" the antics of the WSPU, and "that rowdy scene in the House of Commons".[13] The play sets out to alter misconceptions of suffrage women as "all dowdy and dull" (146) through its "attractive, essentially feminine" heroine, Vida Levering, who, we are told in the stage directions, is "the kind of whom men and women alike say, 'What's her story? Why doesn't she marry?'" (144). One reviewer was puzzled by this mismatch between appearance and political integrity: "Why does she wear such charming frocks? Is it to please other women?", adding that "the cause would make more headway [...] if all its advocates were as fair to look on [...] and as beautifully dressed as Miss Wynne Matthison", the lead actress.[14] By doubling the suffragette heroine with the dramatic figure of the woman with a past, Robins detaches the political woman's "rowdiness" from charges of unsexing. The gradually revealed secret of Vida's decision to abort her unborn child, after being seduced by the Conservative Member of Parliament Geoffrey Stonor 10 years before the action of the play, is not the expected explanation for her problematic single status. Robins is unusual amongst suffrage dramatists in using the "abortion story" of her suffragette heroine to bear on her arguments about unplanned pregnancy, childlessness and political reform in the play. As a dramatist angry at the limited roles for women on the British stage, Robins fitted abortion into her radical critique of male sexuality in order to offer alternative visions of the woman of the future.

This radicalism is toned down in the fictional version of the story, written before Robins was sure of the success of her drama. It is interesting to note that the transformation of the narrative of *Votes for Women!* into a novel, *The Convert*, published later in 1907, resulted in more rally scenes (there are four in total, one of which is the scene of Vida's conversion). This allows her to flesh out the transformative experiences of women in the crowd. This is dramatized in the play through Stonor's fiancée, the childlike Jean Dunbarton, who withdraws her arm from her alarmed lover and presses nearer to the platform before finding her own way through the crowd. Vida's conversion in the novel is described as a mysterious expedition to Trafalgar Square, a place where

> [...] those women, the so-called "Suffragettes", in the intervals of making worse public disturbances, were rumoured to be holding open-air meetings—a circumstance distinctly fortunate for anyone who wanted to "see what they were like" and who was yet unwilling to commit herself.[15]

Attending an organized meeting and taking "those crazy brawlers" seriously is labelled as potentially "compromising" (71), yet the uncommitted reader is also "compromised" in their witnessing of the arguments put forth in favour of citizenship and women's fitness for public affairs. The claiming of the word "suffragette" as a "badge of honour" by one of the speakers—"we accept the clumsy label; we wear it proudly" (89)—may reflect pride in non-violent forms of militancy in the early days of the WSPU.

In the play, there is some confusion about the heroine's status—whether she operates as a militant suffragette or a suffragist who prefers more peaceful methods of protest. Most critics see her as a suffragist, if a rather artificially attractive one, with Penny Farfan criticizing Robins' "tactic of employing the figure of the 'womanly woman' to score feminist points".[16] The debunking of stereotypes about women protesters, however, keeps it ambiguous; though Vida never openly advocates violence, her alignment with Ernestine Blunt, who thanks men for "calling us female hooligans" (173) in the rally scene, may suggest something different. More conservatively, the novel positions Vida's childlessness as problematic by showing her playing with small children and being admonished by her servant for her failure to reproduce: "I've counted a good while on looking after children again some day. But if you won't get married" (34). In the novel, the politically significant process of conversion and the need for women to enter the public sphere is given priority over a critique of motherhood.

This may have something to do with issues of censorship and sexuality. Robins, who signed her name on a letter to *The Times* about the censorship of drama in 1906,[17] was clearly interested in using controversial subject matter and new settings to challenge theatre audiences. *The Times* reviewer was sceptical about the effectiveness of addressing taboo sexual issues in propaganda: "Whether [...] the cause Miss Robins has at heart is likely to be advanced by hanging it onto other questions of seduction, abortion and infanticide is perhaps doubtful".[18] At a time when abortion and infanticide were only referred to obliquely in fiction, they were risky subjects for the stage.[19] Critics such as Sheila Stowell have speculated as to why the director of *Votes for Women!* Harley Granville-Barker's own play, *Waste* (1907), with its abortion references, was refused a licence in the same year that Robins' play was staged in public.[20] Robins had represented an infanticidal mother in the disturbing New Woman play *Alan's Wife* (co-written with Florence

Bell) in 1893, but both women authors felt it prudent to remain anonymous.[21] Smuggling the abortion question into the new genre of suffrage drama, in which the political content might or might not act as a smokescreen for its protest against women's lack of reproductive rights, remained a risk.

"Spectatorship in the theatre", argues Viv Gardner, "is not neutral", particularly at a time when female spectators still did not have the same ease of access to the London theatres as men.[22] The gender dynamics of audiences for suffrage drama have received some attention, particularly in terms of the female matinee crowd with the leisure to occupy theatrical space in the afternoons. Farfan writes of the "sympathetic and predominantly female audience at the Court Theatre", although it is worth pointing out that the extension of the run to evening performances would have made it more open to male spectators.[23] Robins' reputation as an Ibsen actress, coupled with the avant-garde character of the Court Theatre and Granville-Barker as director, might have attracted a more feminist audience; Granville-Barker's advice to change the title from *A Friend of Woman* to *Votes for Women!* (to match the slogan displayed on the banners in Act Two) also put the play's suffrage credentials upfront.[24] The *Era* reviewer suggested that the audience extended beyond supporters of the suffrage by asserting: "if *Votes for Women* does not have the effect of altering opinions as to the question of female suffrage, it will, at any rate, show the women's side of the question in a fresh light to most playgoers".[25] It was risky for women to be seen at both political rallies and at suffrage dramas, as putting themselves forward as spectators in public arenas organized around conversion was potentially compromising. Prepared to court controversy with her subject matter, Robins would certainly have been hoping not only to alter opinions about female suffrage, but also to make her audiences think about how motherhood and unplanned pregnancy affected women's capacities to join the fight.

Motherhood and the "sordid story" of abortion

The controversial subject of abortion needs to be seen in the context of early twentieth-century debates about motherhood and contraception. At a time when the eugenics movement was advocating the sterilization of the unfit in the service of a healthier population, counterarguments about the woman's right to restrict her own fertility were voiced in the radical press. The middle-class woman's access to contraceptive advice before the first birth control clinics in London in the 1920s was limited and incomplete, but the demand for this advice was certainly growing.[26] The tireless campaigner for abortion rights, Stella Browne, encouraged the separation of motherhood from a woman's duty. Her letters to radical periodicals such as Dora Marsden's *The Freewoman* (1911–12) advocated the wider availability of birth control. She argued that "the Woman who is passionately and preeminently maternal shall not be condemned to childlessness through economic pressure and medieval convention, yet our right to refuse maternity is also an invaluable right".[27] These rights of refusal were further articulated in Browne's important pamphlet *Sexual Variety and Variability among Women* (1917), where she claimed that "much actual motherhood is unwilling [...] the underhand opposition to the spread of contraceptive information must be overcome. The ineffably foolish laws penalising abortion must be abolished".[28] However, as Lucy Bland has pointed out, although "most feminists were in favour of sex education as one important element in the long-term solution to male sexual behaviour", many of them recommended chastity rather than birth control.[29] Christabel Pankhurst's modification of the famous slogan "Votes for Women" to "Votes for Women, Chastity for Men" in her *The Great Scourge and How to End It* (1913), which publicized the spread of syphilis in marriage, is an example of this approach.

Suffragist writers pondered the links between maternal status and activism, with some figures attributing their dedication to the cause to their childlessness. In *Marriage as a Trade*, Hamilton identified degradation as the other side of the picture of "the beauty and sanctity of motherhood", and protested against the training of women to be "unintelligent breeding-machines".[30] In her autobiography *Life Errant* (1935), she articulated her childlessness in relation to the ongoing threat of world war, making the choice not to bring children into an unstable society: "I am well content to have no younger generation to fear for".[31] Her celebration of the independence of the single woman seems inseparable from her achievements as a woman writer and activist. In *The Great Scourge*, Pankhurst captures this revaluation of the spinster: "Nowadays the unmarried women have a life full of joy and interest. They are not mothers of children of their flesh, but they serve humanity, they can do work that is beautiful and useful. Therefore their life is complete".[32] Both Hamilton and Pankhurst concur that the singleness of women is valuable for the transformation of society.

Within the context of broader discussions of birth control in the 1900s and 1910s, debates about abortion and unplanned pregnancy were used to mediate a range of feminist arguments about the relationship between women's political helplessness and their lack of control over their fertility. Changing perceptions of the unmarried mother, who was increasingly recognized as a figure in need of feminist help and state support, also influenced this thinking. If the helplessness of women is "[t]he greatest evil in the world" (149), as Vida claimed in the play, then women's helplessness is often shown to stem from unprotected and uninitiated sex. The political arguments in *Way Stations* gathered weight from feminist condemnation of "sex-antagonism", or men's abuses of their sexual power, both within and outside marriage. Robins reflected: "the Suffrage agitation has brought [sex-antagonism] out of hiding [...] The evil of bad relationship between the sexes is not the new thing. The attack upon it is the new thing" (267–68). The consequences of unprotected sex dramatized through the revelations of Vida's secret past in *Votes for Women!* become part of an attack on sex-antagonism by the connections between her individual story and the case histories of wronged women; these were used in the political speeches of the play or passed down from older to younger women in the drawing room.

The passing of stories of seduction between women is framed in terms of hidden knowledge, which the older generation prefer to keep hidden:

> Miss Levering The girls who need shelter and work aren't all serving-maids.
>
> Mrs Heriot (*with an involuntary flash*) We know that all the women who—*make mistakes* aren't.
>
> Miss Levering (*steadily*) That is why every woman ought to take an interest in this—every girl too.
>
> Jean/Lady John (*simultaneously*) Yes—oh, yes!/No. This is a matter for us older—
>
> Mrs Heriot (*with an air of sly challenge*) Or for a person who has some special knowledge. (*Significantly*) *We* can't pretend to have access to such sources of information as Miss Levering.
>
> Miss Levering (*meeting Mrs Heriot's eye steadily*) Yes, for I can give you access. As you seem to think, I have some first-hand knowledge of homeless girls. (151–52)

It is significant that attempts to shield the younger girl from the truth fail here (Lady John's "No" is drowned out), resulting in the suffragist granting access to the ways in which women might make sexual mistakes. The other women associate this first-hand knowledge with "these horrors" (153), though, as in the rally scene, it is important that Jean as a potential convert hears what is usually repressed in polite society. Mrs Heriot later passes the "delicate", "sordid story" onto the "horribly ignorant" girl, who only half understands. The unspeakability of abortion underpins the lending of a large sum of money and the discovery of Vida, "horribly ill", in a lonely Welsh farmhouse, after being visited by a "shady-looking doctor—nameless, of course. And then this result" (154). If abortion is framed as sordid and shameful by the older generation of women, Jean's unexpected response that Vida's campaigning for homeless women should then be seen as a sign of "courage" rather than "effrontery" is significant, given her hidden history; it shows the possibilities for a radical reconfiguration of the next generation's understandings of reproductive rights.

The narratives of seduction, unplanned pregnancy and the risks of prostitution amongst homeless women which circulate in the play demonstrate that female solidarity is needed to raise awareness of sexual dangers. In her

Trafalgar Square speech, Vida's tale of the working girl, who "crawled with the dead body of her new-born child to her master's back-door" (184), before being tried for infanticide by an all-male jury, ends with her acknowledgement of the need for kinship with "our unfortunate sisters" and "every woman who has borne a child" (185). As Joanna Townsend has argued, this is a plea for "co-operation by women with women and for women", as the heroine "is able to connect her experiences of seduction and the maternal body with the more general experiences of women".[33] Drawing on material from Mary Higgs' exposé of destitution and prostitution, *Three Nights in Women's Lodging Houses* (1905), Robins also gives another example of the servant seen dying in a Tramp Ward who becomes a victim of seduction after missing the last train back to her employer's house and "the wrong person found her crying on the platform" (150). However, the concept of shame is reworked in Vida's modification of her seduction narrative as reported to Jean: "All she ever said was that she was ashamed [...] ashamed that she 'hadn't had the courage to resist'—not the original temptation but the pressure brought to bear on her 'not to go through with it'" (154–55). Rejecting the equation of political freedom with "sex freedom" in *The Great Scourge*, Pankhurst proclaimed that women "know too well what is the harvest of wild oats [...] In the opinion of the Suffragettes sex is too big and too sacred a thing to be treated lightly".[34] But Robins retreats from this position of radical celibacy in her play, showing how her heroine remains unashamed of being "tempted" into a sexual affair, and inviting her audience to reject Mrs Heriot's view that an unmarried mother is "not a desirable companion for a young girl" (155). Aligning her with other oppressed mothers who pay the social price for unprotected sex, despite knowing the risks involved, Vida's story also functions as a plea for wider availability of birth control.

In the final act, Robins addresses the complex question of maternal loss in relation to political women's claiming of a voice. Rejecting the pity of society for her lack of husband and child, the suffragist's claim to her own voice becomes inseparable from her rewriting of "her own poor little story": "The only difference between me and thousands of women with husbands and babies is that I'm free to say what I think. *They aren't*" (198; original emphasis). Whilst this again locates freedom of speech with the childless, it seems at odds with Vida's sense of loss in the final confrontation between the former lovers. Sos Eltis has analysed this scene in relation to the text's status as an example of a late "fallen-woman play" in which, "in the hands of a new-woman playwright", the fallen woman evades suicide and shame, her "private grief transmute[d] into political conviction".[35] Vida's often-quoted speech about "one woman's mishap" acquiring broader resonances certainly becomes instrumental in influencing the male politician to vote for women's suffrage: "What general significance has my secret pain? Does it 'join on' to anything?" (207). Yet critics have not paid enough attention to the references to lost maternity in the scene. Within 40 lines, the word "child" recurs 7 times, coupled with notions of sacrifice and wrong. The stage directions indicate her "anguished face", as Stonor, who never knew whether the baby lived or died, is held responsible for the loss: "You can never give me back my child" (207). Maternal anguish is evident in Vida's recalling of the sound of the dead baby crying: "I used to lie there in that lonely farmhouse pretending to hush it. It was so I hushed myself" (203). This traumatic image is followed by her playing of her trump card: "the ghost of a child that had never seen the light, the frail thing you meant to sweep aside and forget" (203), which will instead secure his political support. However, her defiance of his power—"You can't kill this new spirit among women" (205)—implies that her militancy is strengthened because of her loss; the "ventilation" of lost motherhood ensures that her voice is no longer hushed. Her bargaining with him is also couched in terms of the superiority of the childless, with their capacity for political action:

> Since men alone have tried and failed to make a decent world for the little children to live in—it's as well some of us are childless [...] *we* are the ones who have no excuse for standing aloof from the fight. (208; original emphasis)

Such a closing speech, with its emphasis on the "we" suggesting the size of this group, evokes current recoinings of the notion of the childless to the child-free, emptying the term of connotations of failure and lack in order to stress its social and political possibilities.

Militancy and "quiet propaganda" in *Way Stations*

A "readable" and "persuasive" account of the suffrage movement that "takes us [...] into the heart of the conflict",[36] Way Stations maximized its appeal because of the way in which Robins manoeuvred between suffragist and suffragette positions, advocating both "quiet" rebellion and more violent methods such as window-smashing and arson. The American title, referring to local stops along a railway, is linked to its innovative structure.[37] Interwoven with public speeches, letters to the press and articles was one of the first "timetables" of the suffrage movement between 1905 and 1912. Descriptions of events such as imprisonments, parliamentary debates, key speeches and arrests are interspersed with autobiographical fragments under short sections entitled "Time Table". Claire Tylee's misleading classification of the text as political autobiography is less useful than her claim that it was a celebratory "history which prioritises the WSPU", though this label also needs qualifying.[38] In the "Author's Note", Robins casts herself as a hesitant if admiring onlooker at militancy, "never having been one of the more active participants in the events dealt with by this book". However, by reinforcing her "infrequent appearances in print, or on platforms" at times of crisis, this note validates alternative forms of participation. Whilst making no apologies for violence, in "Why", a WWSL pamphlet which also appeared in the journal *Votes for Women* in 1909, she articulates "what passes through the mind of many a quiet, home-keeping, non-militant woman in England to-day" (138),[39] aligning herself with those whose rebellion took other forms. One anonymous American reviewer of *Way Stations* worried that "her zeal for the cause carries her, in the defense of militancy, further than most of us would be willing to follow", but conceded that the work "emphasizes the strength of the woman's movement and makes us feel wholesomely ashamed of ourselves for not knowing more of it than we do".[40] Catering for a range of readers, from members of the WSPU and the WWSL to the quiet, non-militant woman, *Way Stations* is perhaps less a defence of militancy than a recognition of the different ways in which women could participate in the cause.

Shifting understandings of militancy and conversion underpinned the speeches and articles in *Way Stations* written between 1909 and 1912. According to Angela John, who has detailed Robins' habit of dressing up with eloquent words, "her stance on militancy was both clear *and* problematic".[41] By 1912, resurgence in WSPU militant protests, in the form of arson and destruction, prompted public disagreements between Teresa Billington-Grieg of the Women's Freedom League and the Pankhursts. The distinctions between the two societies were sharpened as the Women's Freedom League "endorsed a policy of militancy without violence".[42] Her "Time Table" for November 1912 links the WSPU's damage to property and window-smashing with increased support for the cause. In a particularly pro-WSPU 1912 speech reproduced in *Way Stations*, she locates "the new solidarity among women" (222) and their "indomitable spirit" (223) in more extreme forms of militancy, including law-breaking and violence against property. But this potentially problematic sanctioning of violent militancy is always tempered by a recognition of the cross-class appeal of rebellion, because it allows women to step outside social restrictions. In "Why", she ponders why "women of all classes in England" have felt compelled to join the cause, exposing themselves to danger from the police and showing themselves to be "ready to accept the alienation of many of their friends and most of their menfolk" (102). The following discussion of sweated labour, unequal pay, conditions in workhouses and the injustice of the legal system justifies this acceptance of alienation, because it frees women from the private sphere. She conceives of the "well-bred girls" and "older women" who sell suffrage papers in the streets as not only "bearing witness" to their faith in the cause, but also overturning assumptions that it is only natural for women to shrink from publicity: "So well have women been drilled in the idea that it was undesirable and dangerous for them to do work in public (save as ministrants to pleasure)" (133).

The suffering of mothers and children remains crucial to her defence of militancy in "Why":

> Men in high places continue to advise "quiet propaganda" to women whose friends have grown grey practising quiet methods, to women who know what delay means to wives and mothers in the Potteries, to the shop-girl forced on the streets, to the pallid army of workhouse children. (139)

A 1912 article, "Sermons in Stones" (included in *Way Stations*), protested against the conditions of babies in workhouses who never see the light of day, "the absence of State-trained midwives" (240) and the enforced drudgery of working-class mothers, showing her ongoing commitment to better provision for mothers. In the conclusion to her 1912 speech in the Albert Hall, she appeals for "the help of the ordinary women": "You who have not up to now recognised the need of women's direct share in public affairs—you must see that leaving other women's interests entirely to men is unfair to men, as well as horribly dangerous for women" (254). Robins' distinction between the "open or secret aiders and abettors of Militancy" (270) suggests that there were those who offered support but were unable to declare their sympathies for acts of violence. Her passionate commitment to getting these secret advocates, the ordinary women, to subscribe stemmed from her position as a woman writer, whose interrogation of the meanings of militancy in political speeches, fiction and drama fulfilled the interventionist ideals of the WWSL.

Conclusion

In her "Time Table" for 1908, Robins sets herself apart from "the usual house-party argument and the usual condemnation of militant tactics", preferring to take her place on a cart alongside Mrs Pankhurst in a "rough quarter" (60) of Newcastle. Her own most significant militant tactic was to take up her pen to challenge what she called "drawing-room misrepresentation of the Suffrage scenes" (61). Suffrage drama often revolves around unanswered questions, according to Cockin, resulting in open endings, as "the unresolved conflicts and uneasy tensions in the plays symbolise the problems which could not yet be fully articulated", and the wider social determinants of women's vote-less status.[43] In its confrontation with the taboo subject of abortion, and the lost child that enables political change, *Votes for Women!* raised complex questions about motherhood, militancy and childlessness which are not entirely resolved. By 1913, Robins' protest against "quiet propaganda" remained inseparable from her demands for better conditions for mothers and the ordinary woman. Her radical staging of her militant heroine's struggle to find a voice fit for both the platform and the drawing room resonates with her advice to the WWSL to correct false ideas about women in order to inspire the women writers of the future.

Notes

1. Sandra Stanley Holton, "Reflecting on Suffrage History", *A Suffrage Reader: Changing Directions in British Suffrage History*, ed. Claire Eustance, Joan Ryan, and Laura Ugolini (London: Leicester UP, 2000), pp. 20–36 (29).
2. Claire Eustance, "Meanings of Militancy: The Ideas and Practice of Political Resistance in the Women's Freedom League, 1907–14", *The Women's Suffrage Movement: New Feminist Perspectives*, ed. Maroula Joannou and June Purvis (Manchester: Manchester UP, 1998), pp. 51–64 (59, 62).
3. WWSL leaflet, reproduced in Elizabeth Robins, *Way Stations* (1913; London: Dodo, 2010), p. 82. Subsequent references to *Way Stations* are to this edition and given parenthetically in the text.
4. Angela V. John, *Elizabeth Robins: Staging a Life, 1862–1952* (London: Routledge, 1995), p. 3.
5. Sowon S. Park, "'Doing Justice to the Real Girl': The Women Writers' Suffrage League", Eustance, Ryan, and Ugolini, pp. 90–104 (94).
6. Park, pp. 94, 95.
7. Cicely Hamilton, *Marriage as a Trade* (1909); rpt. in Marie Mulvey Roberts and Tamae Mizuta, eds., *Controversies in the History of British Feminism: The Workers, Women and Labour* (London: Routledge, 1995), pp. 1–250 (225).
8. Hamilton, *Marriage*, p. 236.
9. Naomi Paxton, ed., *The Methuen Drama Book of Suffrage Plays* (London: Bloomsbury, 2013), pp. vii, ix.
10. Katharine Cockin, "Women's Suffrage Drama", Joannou and Purvis, pp. 127–39 (131).
11. Sheila Stowell, *A Stage of Their Own* (Manchester: Manchester UP, 1992), p. 14.
12. Mrs Harlow Phibbs, *The Mother's Meeting* (1913); rpt. in Paxton, pp. 101–06 (101).
13. Elizabeth Robins, *Votes for Women!* (1907); rpt. in Jean Chothia, ed., *The New Woman and Other Emancipated Woman Plays* (Oxford: Oxford UP, 1998), pp. 141–208 (146). Subsequent references are to this edition and given parenthetically in the text.
14. "Review of *Votes for Women!*, by Elizabeth Robins", *The Times*, 10 Apr. 1907: 5.
15. Elizabeth Robins, *The Convert*, ed. Jane Marcus (1907; London: Women's, 1980), p. 71. Subsequent references are to this edition and given parenthetically in the text.
16. Penny Farfan, *Women, Modernism and Performance* (Cambridge: Cambridge UP, 2004), pp. 27, 29.
17. See John, *Elizabeth Robins*, p. 148.
18. "Review of *Votes for Women!*".
19. For a discussion of censorship and indecency in this period, see Celia Marshik, *British Modernism and Censorship* (Cambridge: Cambridge UP, 2006), pp. 1–7.
20. See Stowell, p. 15.
21. For more on the reception of this play, staged at Terry's Theatre in 1893, see John, *Elizabeth Robins*, pp. 87–90.
22. Viv Gardner, "The Invisible Spectatrice: Gender, Geography and Theatrical Space", *Women, Theatre and Performance: New Histories, New Historiographies*, ed. Maggie B. Gale and Viv Gardner (Manchester: Manchester UP, 2000), pp. 25–45 (28).
23. Farfan, p. 32.
24. Stowell, p. 15.

25. "Review of *Votes for Women!* by Elizabeth Robins", *Era*, 13 Apr. 1907: 13.
26. Lesley Hall, "The Suffrage Era, 1902 to 1918", *Outspoken Women: An Anthology of Women's Writing on Sex, 1870–1969*, ed. Hall (London: Routledge, 2005), pp. 37–94 (37).
27. Stella Browne, Letter to *The Freewoman*, 1 Aug. 1912: 217–18.
28. Qtd. in Hall, *Outspoken Women*, pp. 78–79.
29. Lucy Bland, *Banishing the Beast: English Feminism and Sexual Morality, 1885–1914* (Harmondsworth: Penguin, 1995), p. 248.
30. Hamilton, *Marriage*, p. 72.
31. Cecily Hamilton, *Life Errant* (London: J. M. Dent, 1935), p. 286.
32. Qtd. in Hall, *Outspoken Women*, p. 57.
33. Joanna Townsend, "Elizabeth Robins: Hysteria, Politics and Performance", Gale and Gardner, pp. 102–20 (116).
34. Qtd. in Hall, *Outspoken Women*, p. 51.
35. Sos Eltis, "The Fallen Woman on Stage: Maidens, Magdalens, and the Emancipated Female", *The Cambridge Companion to Edwardian Theatre*, ed. Kerry Powell (Cambridge: Cambridge UP, 2000), pp. 222–36 (234).
36. "Review of *Way Stations*, by Elizabeth Robins", *North American Review*, 198.692 (1913): 142.
37. Angela V. John, "Way Stations Revisited", *Women's History Notebooks*, 3.1 (1996): 34–36 (34).
38. Claire Tylee, "Way Stations to Political Wilderness—The Political Autobiography of Elizabeth Robins", *Women's History Notebooks*, 2.2 (1996): 24–37 (28). In her response, John disproved the theory that the text functioned as a political autobiography ("Way Stations", 35).
39. "Why" was then reprinted in *Way Stations*.
40. "Review of *Way Stations*".
41. John, *Elizabeth Robins*, pp. 158, 159.
42. Eustance, p. 59.
43. Cockin, p. 134.

Disclosure statement

No potential conflict of interest was reported by the author.

THE USE OF IRONY AS A SUBVERSIVE ELEMENT IN SUFFRAGE THEATRE

Veronica Pacheco Costa

ABSTRACT
This article seeks to explore how the use of comic irony in suffrage plays might be understood as a subversive element. Pro-suffrage playwrights wrote their propaganda plays in such a way as to ensure that they were funny, mocking and entertaining, whilst at the same time critiquing the social situation of women. Comic irony was used as a tool to convince audiences of the legitimate grievances of women through the use of humour, thereby turning irony into a subversive tool.

Introduction

As we know, in the final few decades of the nineteenth century, women became more involved in public life. The theatre provided one space in which women gained greater visibility, and both writers and performers played a prominent role in the fight for women's rights. Organizations such as the Women Writers' Suffrage League, Actresses' Franchise League (AFL) and The Pioneer Players, a small play-producing subscription society,[1] were established with the aim of linking the literary world with a political agenda. Members of these organizations included eminent playwrights, such as Elizabeth Robins, Edith Craig, Inez Bensusan, Lillah McCarthy, Sybil Thorndike, Vera Holme, Lena Ashwell, Christabel Marshall and Cicely Hamilton, among others. These associations were open to anyone involved in the world of theatre, and they produced and performed plays in favour of women's suffrage.[2] Writing for public performance gave women a powerful voice with an immediate impact. According to Sheila Stowell, the AFL saw in theatre a new medium for propaganda and opened up a section, under the direction of Inez Bensusan, dedicated to reviewing and publishing plays.[3] The strong conviction that political theatre could have a powerful influence is made clear in issue 12 of the suffragist periodical the *Vote*, published in December 1913:

> Miss Cicely Hamilton spoke of the difficulty people of average intelligence experienced in realising entirely new ideas presented to them and said she

> hoped those not already in sympathy with the Women's Movement could be got into the Woman's Theatre even by false pretences, so that they might be convinced by the plays.[4]

The plays did not focus exclusively on the issue of the vote, but instead dealt with other matters of vital importance to women, such as work and their role in society, among other issues. In general, they were short pieces, often monologues, and were intended for performance in the afternoon to a small group of people. The plays were not subversive per se, and they did not constitute aggressive propaganda, which meant that they did not at first glance ward off audiences who were not sympathetic to the suffragist cause. However, their message was clear and direct, and together with the use of irony and humour, they constituted a very powerful subversive discourse.

Some studies, however, perhaps because of the absence of violent protest, do not consider suffrage theatre to have been a powerful element within the suffrage campaign. Barbara Green, for example, states that women used multiple public forums to publicize their campaign and recognizes the theatrical nature of many of their public appearances, but considers that suffrage plays were much less proactive in political terms than other forms of public expression used by the suffrage supporters.[5] As Susan Carlson points out, the fundamental narratives of the suffragettes were based on violence and tragedy, and, in general, literary criticism has focused on theatre of protest or on texts with more clearly political content, leaving the seemingly more conservative texts aside.[6]

This article seeks to build on Stowell's argument that "[t]here is no doubt that suffrage drama was written as part of a consciously organised scheme to propagate political doctrine".[7] It aims to study theatrical texts written by suffragists in which humour and, especially, the use of irony are present, and which have a clearly political role owing to their subversive character. Carlson notes the existence of "comic militancy", which made suffrage plays "politically progressive and socially conservative", and Katharine Cockin states that "an effective means of combating the ideologies which promoted violence was the undermining, deflating power of comedy".[8] Although, as Linda Hutcheon suggests, much of the irony is not necessarily funny,[9] this article attempts to analyse what could be termed "ironic-comic militancy". It will be argued that the comic irony used in these suffrage plays leads to humour and to breaking down the ideological resistance of men and women, which in itself bestows subversive value on the use of irony.

Irony and theatre

The use of irony is not new in theatre. Indeed, of all the literary genres, theatre offers intrinsic elements that facilitate the use of irony—namely, the performative, structural and scenic qualities of theatre itself. As William Storm points out, theatre and its innate characteristics in relation to conflict and dialect make irony its "natural partner", and it can be achieved through dialogue between characters as well as through performance and staging.[10]

One dictionary definition of irony is "the humorous or mildly sarcastic use of words to imply the opposite of what they normally mean [...] used to draw attention to some incongruity or irrationally".[11] The philosopher Socrates, as reflected in Plato's *Dialogues*, before going on to demonstrate his thesis, introduced irony, the purpose of which was to prepare understanding by freeing it of error and prejudice as a prior stage to recognizing the ignorance of his interlocutor and holding him up for ridicule.[12] As this article shows, it would appear that suffragists used irony in their plays to the same end as Socrates.

In her book *Irony's Edge*, Hutcheon begins her introduction with some questions that in themselves are very revealing:

> Why should anyone want to use this strange mode of discourse where you say something you don't actually mean and expect people to understand not only what you actually do mean but also your attitude toward it? How do you decide if an utterance is ironic? In other words, what triggers you to decide that what you heard or saw is not meaningful alone but requires supplementing with a different, inferred meaning (and judgment) that would then lead you to call it irony?[13]

For Hutcheon, there is a series of elements she considers essential for irony to emerge: "its critical edge, its semantic complexity, the discursive communities, the role of intention and its contextual framing and markers".[14] Along the same lines, Burgers, van Mulken and Schellens consider the existence of five elements in irony.[15] Both studies emphasize the need for implicit critical or evaluative criticism of a circumstance, and that this should be recognizable in one way or another by whoever is listening or reading it. This recognition must occur because the literal meaning of irony must be incongruent with what has been mentioned previously, or owing to the context, and in many cases it takes the form of "ironic praise". Finally, irony, it would appear, must necessarily be intentional; in other words, it must be directed at someone and it must in itself contain relevant information for the communicative act.

Given all the elements that make irony possible, S. Attardo distinguishes between "irony factors" and "irony markers", arguing that the former cannot disappear from irony without destroying it, whereas the latter help to detect irony.[16] Burgers, van Mulken and Schellens add further markers such as metaphors, hyperboles and rhetorical questions, repetitions, changes in register, and diminutives, exclamations and tag questions.[17] This article focuses on the analysis of three types of irony: verbal, situational or dramatic, and tactical irony.[18]

To what extent did women make specific use of irony? Irony does appear continuously throughout the history of women's political discourse.[19] According to Tarez Samra Graban, this must be understood as a way of questioning ideology and has proved very useful in feminist rhetoric when redefining the concepts of "agency, language and history".[20] She goes on to note that ironic discourse opens up the possibility for activism to implicitly invite readers to behave as agents in their process of discourse recomposition and relating discourse with other texts and contexts. To her mind, and for the purposes of this article, women have used irony as a tool for humour within a rhetorical and political strategy. As mentioned previously, for irony to exist, there must be intentionality on the part of the person writing it, but there is no doubt that there must be intentionality in the person who receives it, and that individual must be capable of understanding this discourse. In the case of suffrage theatre, irony was captured, obviously, by sympathizers to the cause, and those who were not as sympathetic would be introduced to it in the play through the humour contained within that irony.

Suffrage theatre

In 1908, the AFL held its first meeting in London with the support of renowned actresses of the day such as Ellen Terry, Magde Kendal and Lena Ashwell. As Irene Cockroft and Susan Croft point out, the AFL agreed to support the suffrage cause through the following actions: propaganda meetings, the sale of literature, propaganda plays and lectures.[21] It also agreed to help other associations through what has become known as "sisterhood". Although the association was open to anyone interested in the cause and related in some way to the world of theatre, the executive committee could only be made up of actresses. Cockroft and Croft go on to explain that over the following six years, the AFL worked alongside the Women Writers' Suffrage League, with the AFL taking charge of writing and producing numerous propaganda plays, as well as other activities that helped the suffrage campaigners. For example, since women in general were not accustomed to speaking in public, actresses of the AFL helped to coach them and to develop their public-speaking skills. They also helped women to disguise themselves so as to avoid detention by the police.[22] Unsurprisingly, many members of the AFL were also members of the Women Writers' Suffrage League, including Inez Bensusan, Ellen Terry, Cicely Hamilton, Elizabeth Robins and Christopher St. John, among others. Katherine Kelly suggests that the AFL constructed an identity through its relationship with three institutions: the first was the group of theatre professionals who also had close links with the Ibsen movement and who were regularly involved with associations that promoted the production of plays classed as "new drama"; the second group were pro-suffrage activists, who used their visibility to further the cause, whilst also belonging to a suffrage association; and the third group were, in addition to the above, "Englishwomen" from the middle classes.[23]

The AFL had a special department dedicated to coordinating the writing and production of these plays, the purpose of which was twofold: as propaganda and to raise money. Although some of the plays were dramas, many of them were comedies designed to entertain and inspire undecided people and convert them to the cause.[24] Elaine Aston and Janelle Reinelt point out that the style and content of these plays were largely determined by the political reality of the time. The message should be clear, accessible, educational and entertaining, with a style that Aston and Reinelt term "agripop comic-realism".[25] Shorter plays were published not only in suffrage publications such as the *Vote*, but also in other newspapers and magazines, including the modernist magazine the *New Age*. One of the initiatives of some members of the AFL and the Women Writers' Suffrage League was the play-producing subscription society The Pioneer Players. It was launched in 1911 by Edith Craig, a stage director, actress, producer and designer, together with her partner Christopher St. John and Cicely Hamilton. Cockin claims that it is difficult to define The Pioneer Players' work "because it was an organisation committed to change, to promoting social change and to responding to it, by engaging with controversial current events such as court cases, political campaigns and new legislation".[26] The plays produced and performed by The Pioneer Players dealt with many issues apart from suffrage, such as inequality at work, the disparity in pay between men and women, motherhood and divorce. Cockin points out that "their engagement with political issues surprised and threatened some reviewers, who claimed that they were subversive".[27] Together with this initiative, in May 1913, Inez Bensusan announced in the periodical *Votes for Women* the birth of a "new feminist theatre" based on a cooperative system. This project, known as The Woman's Theatre, was short-lived, since the start of the First World War forced it to become Women's Theatre Camps Entertainments. Kelly notes that, through this initiative, the members of the AFL found a way to commit to peace through war. Even though they performed over 634 entertainments and signed hundreds of artists, the original idea of The Woman's Theatre gradually disappeared, dissolved among the different suffrage factions and the progressive acquisition of rights for women.[28]

With regard to the types of suffrage plays produced and performed, Stowell argues that they offered female playwrights an opportunity to develop their ideas and plays, safe from the limited structures imposed on commercial theatre by the patriarchal hegemony of the age.[29] Thus the theatre gave activists the opportunity to appear in public in a safe environment and to rehearse for their public speeches through a different type of activity.[30] However, in spite of this freedom to write, the plays were in general brief and clear in their subject matter, characterized by realism and naturalism. Suffrage literature in general was not innovative in terms of experimentation in new forms; rather, it was based on the description of events that had taken place in particular activities such as meetings, arrests, protests and strikes. This was clearly a consequence of the ultimate purpose of these plays: propaganda. In fact, many of the plays portrayed the conversion of men and women to the suffragist cause, always maintaining the same social structure so that women were not a threat, and neither were their claims and demands. As Katharine Cockin, Glenda Norquay and Sowon S. Park explain, the setting for many of the plays was the interior of a house, demonstrating the challenge of transferring the political and public landscape to the domestic sphere.[31]

Plays about the fight for the vote

The plays examined in this article contain various examples of the use of irony. The majority of them deal with the issue of suffrage, although without neglecting other issues such as the inequalities between men and women with regard to work and social and family rights, and there is usually a critique of anti-suffrage individuals. One general feature of these plays is the fact that they represented real-life events. *At the Gates*, by Alice Chapin, written in 1909 and published in Susan Croft's *Votes for Women and Other Plays*,[32] is based on actual events and deals with episodes that occurred on a picket line set up by the Women's Freedom League outside the House of Commons between 5 July and 28 October 1909. Croft notes that Chapin was in prison when the play was scheduled to be performed for the first time at London's Royal Albert Hall in December of that year, although eventually it was cancelled due to the lateness of the scheduled performance time. The play portrays some of the episodes that occurred on this picket line and the conversations that took place between a suffragette and sympathizers and non-sympathizers to the cause who were passing by, along with two police officers, some young lads, a drunkard, a seamstress and a Member of Parliament. The backdrop does not change during the play, and theatrical experimentation is minimal. However, verbal irony is patent at various moments as the suffragette talks to the police officers, who are leaving Parliament:

> 1st OFFICER It won't be so late a sitting tonight. It's Arson's Dove-cote Bill. They won't talk so much over it. Last night the budget ran away with them.
>
> SUFFRAGETTE I wish it had run so far they couldn't find their way back.
>
> 2nd OFFICER Bit nippy tonight, don't you think?
>
> SUFFRAGETTE Yes, it seems frosty.
>
> 2nd OFFICER It's wonderful how cold it gets down here. The wind over the river, I suppose.

1st OFFICER You won't be able to stand the really cold weather, Miss. It is too much for us sometimes.

SUFFRAGETTE Unless a microbe penetrates to the brain of one in authority, I shall have to stand it.[33]

At this point, several Members of Parliament arrive, including one named Merrypebble, about whom the suffragette remarks: "Tarnished, disgraced by its present possessor. Why, when his policy rouses a storm he doesn't dare to face the music himself. He leaves a Secretary to do it for him. He has not even the courage of his convictions". From these comments about this politician, she moves onto another, claiming that "he has more brains in his little finger than any of the rest of them have in their whole bodies".[34] While the two police officers and the suffragette continue to stand by the gates to Parliament, various other characters begin to appear onstage. The first is a male sympathizer who is interested in and supports the cause, and who serves the propagandistic purposes of the play by way of an example of a pro-suffrage man. In the middle of the conversation/propaganda between the sympathizer and the suffragette, there is the voice of another person passing by, who says "Votes for Women, I don't think", to which the suffragette responds ironically, echoing his last words: "No, you look as if you didn't".[35] The sympathizer, accompanied by a waiter, takes tea to the suffragette, who talks to the two police officers and the sympathizer about the Members of Parliament who are leaving Parliament, in a conversation that includes a heavy dose of irony and even a rhyme on the part of the suffragette:

1st OFFICER I am not. Not one has escaped me. Five have bowed.

SYMPATHIZER Five? Oh, that's something.

SUFFRAGETTE Yes, they will learn manners in time. At least some of them will. Some still find it amusing to see a woman standing at these gates. They evidently forget that we pay taxes for the upkeep of all this, and that we are seriously influenced by some of their stupid laws. Still, five remember us. We can afford to be hopeful. Five little men, we can count on now, five little men, who don't forget to bow.

SYMPATHIZER (wickedly) Perhaps they didn't bow, only ducked.[36]

Later, a seamstress approaches the picket line and gives the suffragette her full support, even though it does not count for anything. The seamstress tells the suffragette that her husband hits her, and adds ironically: "Made me a nice object, didn't he?" She complains that the magistrate barely even remonstrated with him for it, and only told him not to do it again—advice that the husband chose to ignore. She also speaks of her poor working conditions and the need for women to have more rights. The next character to enter is an older lady, who states forcefully "I am a womanly woman", as she holds her parasol, adjusts her hat and walks away majestically to catch a taxi. When faced with this show of stereotypical middle-class femininity, the suffragette creates situational irony, stating: "These antis are so militant". The next character is a man who says the same thing as the drunkard—"Votes for women, isn't it? I think not"—and the suffragette remarks ironically: "I've heard something like that remark before". At the end of a long speech, the man, who reproaches the suffragette, saying that she is making money through her protests whereas he has no money, states: "I am a man, too. You are not a man"—a phrase used by the suffragette to retort ironically: "Thank God for that!" One of the police officers moves him along because he is starting to become bothersome, but before he leaves he says: "I am a gentleman, I am a gentleman, I am-I am a voter. She can't vote, and while I have my way, she shan't". This leads the police officer to describe with irony:

1st OFFICER Nice specimen that of the free and independent.

SUFFRAGETTE Yes, I wonder which party he belongs to.

2nd OFFICER To the one that gives him the most beer.[37]

The play ends with the suffragette chatting to a Member of Parliament who has approached her. After he has commented ironically on the obstinacy of the suffragettes, mentioning the violent acts of some women and the action of the police, the Member of Parliament says that he must go back into Parliament.

Another play that portrays typical suffragist discourse, *Votes for Women*, was written by Elizabeth Robins in 1907. Robins' play focuses on the evolution of Miss Levering in the private and public spheres, and it opens with a group of upper-class wives dedicated to organizing charitable acts, whose husbands are very busy and devoted to their professional careers. The portrait painted by Robins of these wives, who are more concerned with the mundane, contrasts with the suffrage activism of Vida Levering and a young idealist, Jean Dunbarton, who discovers that, beyond the living rooms of high society, there is a world to fight for. According to Croft: "Robins challenges the stereotype of the dowdy, unattractive feminist and the conventional demand that the fallen woman be made to suffer for her sins".[38] In Act One, Miss Levering becomes embroiled in an ironical dialogue, containing situational and content irony, with Greatorex, a Member of Parliament, and the young Jean:

GREATOREX The great mistake was in teaching them to read and write.

JEAN (over Miss Levering's shoulder, whispers) Say something.

MISS LEVERING (to Greatorex smiling) Oh no, that wasn't the worst mistake.

GREATOREX Yes, it was.

MISS LEVERING No, believe me. The mistake was in letting women learn to talk.[39]

In Act Two, the character of a suffrage campaigner called Ernestine Blunt appears, giving a speech in the street, where she is questioned by the people who gather round her. This situation gives rise to various ironic moments in the content, and also through the italicization of certain words where the actress must give emphasis or use a special tone of voice to draw the attention of the audience watching the play. All of these ironic-comic interactions, as well as the political message, come across clearly and directly:

> MISS ERNESTINE BLUNT If we didn't know by any other sign, the comic papers would tell us we've arrived! But our greatest debt of gratitude we owe, to the man who called us female hooligans … (the crowd bursts into laughter) … We aren't hooligans, but we hope the fact will be overlooked. If everybody said we were nice, well-behaved women, who'd come to hear us? Not the men. (roars) Men tell us it isn't womanly for us to take care about politics. How do they know what's womanly? It's for women to decide that. Let the men attend to being manly. It will take them all their time.[40]

At the end of the play, Miss Levering also takes to the stand to speak, thereby moving from silence to speaking out not only in public, but also to resolve private matters from her past.[41] Her discourse is interrupted by a man who asks her if there are any women magistrates, or a female Beethoven or Shakespeare, to which Levering answers ironically that there are also no such illustrious figures among men:

> How many Platos are there in this crowd? […] Not one. Yet that doesn't keep you men off the register. […] Yet the State doesn't tumble into pieces. Railroads and ships are built, homes are kept going and babies are born. The world goes on. It goes on by virtue of its common people.[42]

The consequences of women not having the vote are dealt with extensively in the play *How the Vote Was Won*, written in 1909 by Cicely Hamilton and Christopher St. John.[43] This hit comedy "focuses on the dilemma for capitalism and patriarchy",[44] and portrays the conversion of a family patriarch at the end of the play. The plot revolves around the situation that all the women throughout the country have stopped working and have started to behave like kept women, demanding to be maintained by the man of the family. And so Horace's house becomes filled with female relatives who have left their jobs and demand to be maintained. This comic premise provokes various ironic-comic situations within the political message. As in Robins' play, the setting is conservative—the parlour of a middle-class home with two servants, which is not at all unfamiliar for audience members who are undecided about the suffrage cause. When Horace's sister, Agatha, arrives at the house, Horace's wife, Ethel, is surprised to see her there and does not understand what has happened, saying that she thought Agatha was happy working for the Lewis family. Agatha responds in an ironic tone as she criticizes her working conditions: "So were the slaves in America when they had kind masters. They didn't want to be free". Horace reproaches her for having become a suffrage supporter when she seemed to be a lady, to which Ethel responds ironically: "Yes, I was a lady, such a lady that at eighteen I was thrown upon the world, penniless, with no training whatever which fitted me to earn my own living".[45]

The second female relative to arrive at Horace's house is Molly, his niece, who says as soon as she enters: "Cheer up, Uncle. Now's your chance to reform me. I've come to live with you. You can support me and improve me at the same time". The third relative is Christine, whom Horace does not even recognize. The fourth relative is Maudie, a distant cousin, who comes in singing an ironic song: "A woman's place is in the home, I don't think, I don't think". Finally, Horace realizes how ridiculous it is not to give women the vote and quickly converts to the cause of women's suffrage. Together with his female relatives and some other men, he takes to the streets calling for votes for women.[46]

Although this play is comic and also contains examples of irony, the consequences of not having the vote are also shown in non-comic plays, such as *Change of Tenant* by Helen Margaret Nightingale, written in 1908.[47] In the play, the owner of a house, Squire Brooks, is considering no longer renting the house to the widow Mrs Basset, who has been living there for over 30 years, because, although she is a good tenant, since she does not have the right to vote, she will be unable to support Brooks' son in the elections. Brooks has an offer to rent from a man, John Smith, which is more beneficial for his purposes. Mrs Basset does not stay at home and decides to go and speak with Brooks, and convince him not to terminate her rental contract on the grounds that she is a woman. The ironic moments come when Brooks speaks to the audience behind Smith's back, ridiculing him.

Plays about the image of anti-suffrage women versus suffragists

One of the subjects that offers the most examples of irony is the comic representation of anti-suffrage women, their behaviours and strategies, and even the way they dress, just as anti-suffrage women attacked suffrage campaigners. Naomi Paxton, in *The Methuen Drama Book of Suffrage Plays*, includes the four plays being analysed here. The first is by Beatrice Harraden: *Lady Geraldine's Speech*, written in 1909. The story takes place in the parlour of Harraden's childhood friend and suffragist Dr Alice Romney. Lady Geraldine pays her a visit to ask for her help in writing a speech for the Anti-Suffrage League. Alice agrees to help her and, as she writes the speech, various suffrage friends appear in the parlour. The comic irony of this play is situational, since a suffragist is writing an anti-suffrage speech and, naturally, her suffragist friends make various ironic comments throughout the course of the play. The general image of the suffragists portrayed in this play is that of a group of happy, intelligent women with a good sense of humour, and even Lady Geraldine, the anti-suffragist, is portrayed as a charming lady, albeit a little confused.[48] The first friend to arrive at the house is Silberthwaite, an important artist, who thinks that Alice is writing a pro-suffrage speech, which evidently causes all kinds of misunderstandings and ironic moments throughout the play. One example is the line Silberthwaite speaks to Lady Geraldine when the latter confesses that she is nervous about her first ever speech: "Ah, well, we all have to go through that. But it's worthwhile for the sake of the Cause, isn't it?" The next friend to arrive is Baillie, a literature professor who remarks to Silberthwaite and Lady Geraldine that she is sure Chaucer would have demanded votes for women. The next friend is Hilda Crowninshield, a famous painter, followed by Nellie Grant, a writer. With all the friends gathered together in the parlour, the comedy reaches its peak, since they all believe that Lady Geraldine is a suffragist, which gives rise to various examples of tactical irony:

> BAILLIE I really do think that the antis are our best friends.
>
> LADY GERALDINE Why? I don't quite understand. I should have thought they were very formidable foes.
>
> SILBERTHWAITE Oh dear, no! You needn't have any fears about that. You see, with a few exceptions, they can't speak—they haven't had the practice—they haven't learnt how to hold an audience.[49]

But the confusion clears up when Lady Geraldine, whose anti-suffrage convictions are gradually weakened, tells them that she is anti-suffrage. The other women are not riled or angry; instead, they remark on the situation ironically:

> SILBERTHWAITE Great Heavens! How delightful! I've been longing to meet one face to face. No one brought me the anti-suffrage petition.

The one exception is Alice, who defends Lady Geraldine and says she is her best childhood friend. Alice's explanation about the speech she has written for Lady Geraldine is filled with irony:

> Well, now for the speech, Geraldine. I've quite enjoyed this little job. I'm rather pleased with it. I think I've brought in all the points. Degradation of Womanhood. Degradation and disintegration of the entire Empire. Dominant female vote in all matters concerning the Army and the Navy, our relations with foreign Powers, with our Colonies, and with India. Physical force argument. Women have to safeguard the past and the future, and it is the men's work to look after the present. I don't myself know what that means, but it sounds

> well. [...] A few passing allusions to us suffragists as obscure vulgarians. I think you might almost call us uneducated.[50]

It is no accident that Alice adds to the anti-suffrage speech she gives to her friend that suffragists are "uneducated". In fact, one of the main pillars of the suffrage movement was the importance of education as a tool to empower women.[51] A further example of situational irony is the fact that the person who utters this phrase has a doctorate and is at that moment surrounded by highly educated and qualified women. Another play that highlights the importance of education is undoubtedly *A Pageant of Great Women* (1910), by Cicely Hamilton.[52] This play brings a list of important and educated women who are demanding freedom together with warriors, saints, queens and heroines to such an extent that "the ending appears to contemplate unrestricted possibilities for women".[53] Cockin argues that Hamilton and Craig "packed the stage with women portraying historical precedents as evidence for the merits of women's enfranchisement and reactivating the tense political reverberations".[54] These two works are, in turn, highly educational, since they show the existence of important "educated" women.

The comedy by Cicely Hamilton and Cristopher St. John, *Pot and Kettle*, from 1909, once again ridicules anti-suffrage women and offers a peaceable image of suffragists and their political campaign.[55] In this case, Marjorie, an anti-suffrage girl from a good family, gets into a fight with a suffragist, the daughter of a marquis, who has accused Marjorie of hitting her. Marjorie's parents, in a state of shock, ask their suffragist niece, Nell, to talk to her upper-class fellow suffragist and ask her to withdraw this accusation. The examples of irony in this play usually come from the responses of Nell, as in, for example, when Marjorie describes the marquis's suffragist daughter, whom she hit:

> MARJORIE She had on a fawn coat and a black hat with daisies in it; but she was really a suffragette—though I didn't know. She looked just like anyone else.
>
> NELL Some of us do. Go on.[56]

When, at the end of the play, Nell resolves the problem and convinces her fellow suffragist to withdraw her accusation, the process of conversion appears once again, presenting suffragists as peaceful women.

The conversion process can also be an act of self-recognition of ideological positions of which a character had not previously been aware, reaching people who had not realized they were pro-suffrage but are "awoken" when they come into contact with anti-suffragism. This is the case in *Miss Appleyard's Awakening* (1911), a play by Evelyn Glover. Here, irony is situational, since Miss Appleyard does not consider herself a suffragist, but over the course of the play, through the conversations she has with the anti-suffrage Miss

Crabtree and her refusal to sign the anti-suffrage pamphlet, Miss Appleyard realizes her pro-suffrage ideas. She even ends up saying to Miss Crabtree: "It seems to me that you want every woman to be a perfect tool!"[57] In the monologue written by Mrs Harlow Phibbs, *The Mother's Meeting* (1913), comic irony comes from the mispronunciations and mistakes of Mrs Puckle, such as "[t]he woman's fear is the ome",[58] which ironically sounds like "the woman's sphere is the home", thereby comparing the domestic sphere with fear.

Plays about the problems faced by women in the workplace

The problems faced by women in the workplace were another major subject tackled in suffrage plays, such as the comedy *Diana of Dobson's* (1908), by Cicely Hamilton. Diana is working as a shop assistant in a major department store when she receives a letter telling her that she is to inherit £300 after the passing of a distant cousin. Diana decides to spend the money on something she will remember, such as travelling and enjoying her freedom for a month. To this end, she invents a new identity for herself, becoming the widow Massingberg and travelling to Switzerland. This play on identity has a comic effect on the audience and also serves as a resource for the use of tactical irony—for example, when Diana states: "I don't know I should describe myself as a great walker, but I'm used to being on my feet all day".[59] Another example is when she runs out of money and, as an excuse for leaving the hotel in Switzerland, says: "It was only this morning I found out it would be necessary for me to start today".[60] This comedy stands in sharp contrast to the drama of a group of seamstresses in Edith Lyttelton's play *Warp and Woof* (1904), in which one of the workers, Phoebe, gets very sick due to hard work.[61]

As for inequalities at work and the presumption that women are inferior to men, Elizabeth Baker's play *Edith* (1912) provides another clear example of comic irony.[62] In this play, Edith's father has died, and the family get together to read the will. The surprise comes when they find out that the father has left the business to his daughter and not to his son, as expected. Edith appears almost at the end of the play as a true success story, since she is not a shop assistant, as everyone assumes, but rather the owner of a chain of stores. There is dramatic irony when the family start out by describing her as "a mere girl, just a girl"[63] and are eventually convinced of her intelligence and capacity to run the business. In the volume of texts edited by Cockin, Norquay, and Park, there are two plays in which the inequality between men and women is made evident. The first is a drama by Bessie Hatton, *Before Sunrise* (1909), which shows the tragedy of marriage for many girls whose dreams were not to become a wife, as well as the lack of understanding shown by their families, who see marriage as the only possible future for their daughters. In spite of the drama, we find an example of irony in the phrase uttered by the mother of the girl who is being forced to marry, when she says: "I know that men won't marry clever women, and I for one don't blame them".[64] The irony resides in the fact that she is classing herself as a silly woman, which discredits all her actions. In this play, the daughter's own mother is her worst enemy, and this fact—that women are the first ones who have to reflect on their role in society—is also the subject of Gertrude Jennings' play, *A Woman's Influence.* (1912)[65] The play opens with Margaret trying to convince her husband, Herbert, to talk to Mr Reed to improve the living conditions for the female workers in a factory. A widowed friend, Mrs P., manages to get his attention by using stereotypical female behaviour, playing dumb and flattering the man, but when she realizes she has money invested in the factory, she backtracks and asks Herbert not to do anything. The husband and wife realize what is happening and, in the end, Herbert helps his wife. The irony of this play is tactical because the widow deceives and conceals information that she shares with the audience.

Conclusions

I have intentionally left one play to discuss in this closing section. In my opinion, it is one of the most representative examples of the subversive effect of irony in suffrage theatre. The play is *The First Actress* (1911), by Christopher St. John, which offers an example of meta-theatre along with situational and dramatic irony throughout.[66] Set in 1611, it is about a theatre company and the impossibility of women acting onstage at that time. The crowning ironic moment in the play comes in the final speech, as the characters talk about the fact that, in due course, the whole world will laugh when it finds out that women were not allowed to act on the stage. The play seeks to compare this with the current moment when everyone laughs as they find out that women are not allowed to vote, and this irony forces us to reflect on how things can change, whilst also tying in the struggles of the past with the present.

Cockin explains that the representation of women as writers and performers, as in *The First Actress*, "exposed the limits of the separate-sphere ideology", and she states that writing was perceived by suffragists to be a political act, but even more important was the fact that women were reclaiming the power of speech as a way to conquer the male sphere of public life.[67] Unsurprisingly, in this same regard, Cicely Hamilton claimed that "one play is worth one hundred speeches", which clearly shows that she was aware of the tremendous power of theatre.[68]

This article has analysed the comic-ironic elements used in some suffrage plays as tools to demolish prejudice and error, as Socrates proposed, and to explore problems and spark debate about the working situation of women, their enfranchisement and the right of women to be citizens, among the other concerns suffragists had. As we have seen throughout this article, the use of comic irony is a key element in these suffrage plays that, set against a conservative backdrop and in the absence of theatrical experimentation, was turned into a subversive element, which was imperceptible but effective in the transmission of pro-suffrage political ideas.

Notes

1. Katharine Cockin, *Women and Theatre in the Age of Suffrage: The Pioneer Players, 1911–1925* (London: Palgrave, 2001), p. 9.
2. Susan Croft, ed., *Votes for Women and Other Plays* (London: Aurora Metro, 2009), p. 10.
3. Sheila Stowell, *A Stage of Their Own: Feminist Playwrights of the Suffrage Era* (Ann Arbor: U of Michigan P, 1992), p. 42.
4. The Vote, 12, December 1913. pp. 117–118.
5. Barbara Green, *Spectacular Confessions: Autobiography, Performative Activism and the Sites of Suffrage 1905–1938* (New York: St. Martin's, 1997), p. 15. See also Jane Eldridge, *Rebel Women: Feminism, Modernism and the Edwardian Novel* (London: Virago, 1994), p. 131.
6. Susan Carlson, "Comic Militancy: The Politics of Suffrage Drama", *Women, Theatre and Performance: New Histories, New Historiographies*, ed. Maggie B. Gale and Viv Gardner (Manchester: Manchester UP, 2000), pp. (198–215).
7. Stowell, p. 439.
8. Carlson, p. 208; Katharine Cockin, *Edith Craig and the Theatres of Art* (London: Bloomsbury, 2017), p. 102.
9. Linda Hutcheon, *Irony's Edge* (London: Routledge, 1994), p. 4.
10. William Storm, *Irony and the Modern Theatre* (Cambridge: Cambridge UP, 2011), p. 11.
11. Collins Dictionary, Harper Collins Publisher, 1991. pp. 536
12. W. K. C. Guthrie, *Socrates* (Cambridge: Cambridge UP, 1971).
13. Hutcheon, p. 2.
14. Hutcheon, p. 4.
15. Christian Burgers, Margot van Mulken, and Peter Jan Schellens, "Verbal Irony: Differences in Usage across Written Genres", *Journal of Language and Social Psychology*, 31.3 (2012): 290–310.
16. S. Attardo, "Irony Makers and Functions: Towards a Goal-Oriented Theory of Irony and Its Processing", *Rask*, 12 (2000): 3–20.
17. Burgers, 295.
18. Some authors identify up to 15 types of irony. See, for example, D. C. Muecke, *Irony and the Ironic: The Critical Idiom* (London: Methuen, 1970).
19. Robert Coles, *Irony in the Mind's Life: Essays on Novels by James Agee, Elizabeth Brown and George Elliot* (Charlottesville: U of Virginia P, 1974), p. 20.
20. Tarez Samra Graban, *Women's Irony: Rewriting Rhetorical Histories* (Carbondale: Southern Illinois UP, 2015), p. 5.
21. Irene Cockroft and Susan Croft, *Art, Theatre and Women's Suffrage* (London: Aurora Metro, 2010), p. 46.
22. Elaine Aston and Janelle Reinelt, *Modern British Women Playwrights* (Cambridge: Cambridge UP, 2000), p. 4.

23. Katherine E. Kelly, "The Actress Franchise League Prepares for War: Feminist Theatre in Camouflage", *Theatre Survey*, 35.1 (1994): 121–37 (121).
24. Croft, pp. 11, 12.
25. Aston and Reinelt, pp. 4, 5.
26. Cockin, *Women*, p. 10.
27. Cockin, *Women*, p. 6.
28. Kelly, 129.
29. Stowell, pp. 66, 67.
30. Katharine Cockin, Glenda Norquay, and Sowon S. Park, eds., *Women's Suffrage Literature*, 6 vols. (London: Routledge, 2007), vol. 1, p. iv.
31. Cockin, Norquay, and Park, vol. 1, p. iv; vol. 3, p. ix.
32. Croft, pp. 121–38.
33. Croft, p. 124.
34. Croft, pp. 125, 126.
35. Susan Croft's Votes for Women and Other Plays, pp. 126
36. Croft, p. 130.
37. Croft, pp. 134–135.
38. Croft, p. 22.
39. Croft, p. 51.
40. Croft, p. 65.
41. Joanna Townsend, "Elizabeth Robins: Hysteria, Politics and Performance", Gale and Gardner, pp. (102–120).
42. Croft, p. 77.
43. The play is published in Katharine Cockin, ed., *Women's Suffrage Literature*, vol. 3 (London: Routledge, 2007), pp. 135–170.
44. Cockin, *Edith*, p. 103.
45. Cockin, *Women's Suffrage*, p. 153.
46. Cockin, *Women's Suffrage*, pp. 165–68.
47. The play is published in Croft, pp. 109–118.
48. Naomi Paxton, ed., *The Methuen Drama Book of Suffrage Plays* (London: Bloomsbury, 2014), p. xii.
49. Paxton, pp. 37–41.
50. Paxton, pp. 42–44.
51. Cockin, vol. 3, p. x.
52. The play is published in Cockin, Norquay, and Park, vol. 1, vol. 3, pp. 189–265.
53. Katharine Cockin, "Cicely Hamilton's Warriors: Dramatic Reinventions of Militancy in the British Women's Suffrage Movement", *Women's History Review*, 14.3–4 (2005): 527–42.
54. Cockin, *Edith*, p. 65.
55. Paxton, p. xii.
56. Paxton, p. 59.
57. Paxton, p. 84.
58. Paxton, p. 102.
59. The play is published in Fidelis Morgan, *The Years Between: Plays by Women on the London Stage 1900–1950* (London: Virago, 1994), pp. 5–59.
60. Morgan, p. 37.
61. The play is published in Maggie B. Gale and Gilli Bush-Baily, eds., *Plays and Performance Texts by Women 1880–1930* (Manchester: Manchester UP, 2012), pp. 155–206.
62. The play is published in Gale and Bush-Baily, pp. 278–291.

63. Plays and Performance Texts by Women (1880–1930. Edited by B. Gale & Gilli Bush-Bailey. Manchester University Press, 1988. pp. 281
64. Cockin, Norquay, and Park, vol. 3, pp. 395–418. (401).
65. Cockin, Norquay, and Park, vol. 3, pp. 419–442.
66. The play is published in Cockin, Norquay, and Park, vol. 3, pp. 3–23.
67. Katharine Cockin, "Women's Suffrage Drama", *The Women's Suffrage Movement: New Feminist Perspectives*, ed. Maroula Joannou and June Purvis (Manchester: Manchester UP, 1998), pp. 127–39.
68. Cited in Julie Holledge, *Innocent Flowers: Women in the Edwardian Theatre* (London: Virago, 1981), p. 123.

Disclosure statement

No potential conflict of interest was reported by the author.

ORCID

Veronica Pacheco Costa http://orcid.org/0000-0002-6561-9571

THE AMERICAN SUFFRAGE MOVEMENT AND THE NOVELS OF MARIETTA HOLLEY AND ELIA PEATTIE AS A MEANS OF CULTURAL LOBBYING

Emine Geçgil

ABSTRACT
Women's literary activity during the first two decades of the twentieth century, fuelled by the progressive spirit, served as a form of cultural lobbying through which they could articulate social and political problems and propose solutions. This article focuses on the struggle that enfranchised women by examining two long-forgotten suffrage novels, written in a period when grass-roots activism, suffrage parades and house-to-house canvassing were a means of propaganda: Marietta Holley's *Samantha on the Woman Question* (1913) and Elia Peattie's *The Precipice* (1914). With her use of satire, Holley familiarizes her middle-class audience with women's suffrage and politics. By presenting the plight of different women in a vernacular style, Holley addresses the older generation of anti-suffragist women, illuminating how countless unfortunate women are oppressed by a political system that does not acknowledge their presence. On the other hand, in *The Precipice*, Elia Peattie appeals to the younger generation of New Women, portraying the life of a twentieth-century social reformer, who tries to balance her career as a municipal housekeeper with the traditional roles and values of her day. The article argues that both novels functioned as catalysts to bring about social change at a time when, on the federal level at least, women still could not vote or hold an elected office. Thus, even before women were enfranchised, these novels influenced the beliefs and opinions of female audiences, for whom reading fiction was a favourable pastime. Without marginalizing female protagonists or blatantly alienating readers by transgressing socially accepted gender norms, these authors were able to find a middle ground, successfully creating role models who try to change society from within. By rendering the New Woman unthreatening, they challenged the ideology of separate spheres and prepared the public for the great changes ahead.

During the Progressive Era, a widespread concern over social justice unavoidably shaped American politics. Although progressive women played a prominent role in the regulatory policies enacted, they remained peripheral to the progressive movement as they had not attained their political rights—in particular, the right to vote. By virtue of their domestic roles as housekeepers and nurturers, they served as municipal housekeepers,[1] moral guardians[2] and labour agitators. They required the suffrage, however, in order to become active participants and decision-makers in American political life, and to become far more visible in the public sphere. Only in this way would the transition from True Womanhood to New Womanhood be complete.

This article focuses on the struggle that enfranchised American women by examining two suffrage novels: Marietta Holley's *Samantha on the Woman Question* (1913) and Elia Peattie's *The Precipice* (1914).[3] Both novels shed light on an eventful episode in American women's history, when much of the activism took place in the form of lobbying, suffrage parades and house-to-house canvassing. Both novelists allude to the real events that took place at the time they were written to clarify their goals. However, their styles as novelists are different. Where Holley embraces folksy humour to make satiric points, Peattie adopts the more conventional style of a romantic novelist. With her use of satire, Holley familiarizes her middle-class audience with women's suffrage and politics through Samantha's trip to Washington, DC. On the other hand, in *The Precipice*, Peattie appeals to the younger generation of New Women, portraying the life of a twentieth-century social reformer, who tries to balance her career as a municipal housekeeper with the traditional roles and values of her day. Both novels take a mainstream, middle-class, progressive stance. While *Samantha on the Woman Question* exposes the plight of uneducated rural women who are deprived of their political rights, *The Precipice* depicts the modern and purposeful woman as she fights for social change and legal reform, specifically in the realm of suffrage. Both novels disseminated pro-suffrage arguments, serving as vehicles to bring about social change, and inviting middle-class audiences to participate in the suffrage movement without transgressing socially accepted gender boundaries.

Undoubtedly, the transition from True Woman to New Woman was facilitated by suffrage organizations. The National American Woman Suffrage Association (NAWSA) was the most important suffrage organization in the United States. It was established in 1890 through the merger of two rival suffrage societies: the National Woman Suffrage Association and the American Woman Suffrage Association.[4] Under the leadership of Susan B. Anthony, the aim of the NAWSA was to welcome all women—despite their differences—to work for the cause to enfranchise women. While the NAWSA continued to lobby for both statewide enfranchisement and a national amendment to the US constitution,[5] Harriot Stanton Blatch, Alice Paul and Lucy Burns introduced the militancy of the British suffragettes to the American suffrage movement.[6] They founded the Congressional Committee, an auxiliary to the NAWSA, as a platform to engage in *mild* militancy in support of a national amendment. They organized a suffrage parade in March 1913, the day before the inauguration of Woodrow Wilson as president. The event became even more sensational when a large crowd of onlookers assaulted the marchers, and the police did little to intervene.[7] Nevertheless, the event succeeded in reintroducing the suffrage amendment to the House of Representatives, focusing national attention on the cause.

Women's literary activity, fuelled by the progressive spirit of the era, served as a form of cultural lobbying through which they could articulate social and political problems, and propose solutions. Despite all the ideological and methodological differences, countless women writers contributed to the suffrage movement by writing fiction that targeted white, Protestant, middle-class audiences. A prominent suffragist and the co-founder of Virginia's Equal Suffrage League (with Ellen Glasgow), Mary Johnston (1870–1936), took an active part in parades and addressed state legislatures to promote the cause. Her novel *Hagar* (1910) exposes the tensions between the southern lady and the New Woman.[8] In an attempt to promote California's suffrage campaign, Gertrude Atherton (1857–1948), a well-known woman novelist, wrote both fiction and non-fiction to support the cause. Her novel *Julia France and Her Times* (1912) chronicles the life of Julia France, a beautiful American woman of the high elite circles, who joins the Woman's Social and Political Union in the United Kingdom to escape from marriage. Similarly, Elizabeth Robins (1862–1952), an actress and novelist, was drawn into the British suffrage movement while residing in England, and her best-known play, *Votes for Women!* (1907), the first suffrage drama, was subsequently turned into a novel, *The Convert* (1907). This became inspirational for the militant suffrage campaigners in the United States, who were disturbed by the moderate tactics performed by the NAWSA. The novel served as a propaganda tool in both labour and suffrage movements as it evoked cross-class sisterhood, bringing elite women and working-class women together. Undoubtedly, the first two decades of the twentieth century witnessed many other writers whose novels aimed to educate their readers in the realm of suffrage, to increase their enthusiasm, and to publicize particular state campaigns throughout the country. These novels were so influential that they became instrumental in shaping the ideology of their readers, and thereby helped to bring change.

Marietta Holley and the women's suffrage movement

Marietta Holley was a courageous woman writer who took up the male enterprise of satire, which was considered to be a political and socially "dangerous" literary form for women in the nineteenth century.[9] In 1873, she published the satiric work *My Opinions and Betsy Bobbet's* under the "non-threatening" pseudonym "Josiah Allen's Wife".[10] In her own words, she wrote the novel because "[t]he great subject of Wimmen's Rites kept a goarin' me, and a voice kept a sayin' inside of me, 'Josiah Allen's Wife, write a book givin' your views on the great subject of Wimmen's Rites'".[11] With *My Opinions and Betsy Bobbet's*, Holley launched her "Samantha" series, which portrayed the adventures of the Allens, including Samantha, who leaves her fictional town of Jonesville to raise awareness about a social injustice. The Samantha series was so popular at the time the books were published that they sold millions of copies in the United States.[12] Holley, through the character of Samantha, criticizes Mormon polygamy in *The Lament of the Mormon Wife* (1880), while *Sweet Cicely: Josiah Allen as a Politician* (1885) is a temperance novel portraying the plight of women suffering from drunken husbands and fathers.[13] With *Samantha at Saratoga* (1887), she focuses on dress reform, whereas *Samantha among the Brethren* (1890) calls for church reform.[14] *Samantha on the Race Problem* (1892) addresses the white-slave traffic, American imperialism, xenophobia and race antagonism, while *Samantha at the World's Fair* (1893), *Samantha in Europe* (1896), *Samantha at the St. Louis Exposition* (1904) and *Around the World with Josiah Allen's Wife* (1905) familiarize the late Victorian True Woman with the outside world.[15] With *Samantha on Children's Rights* (1909),[16] Holley writes about children whose mothers need the ballot in order to protect them from harsh labour conditions, and to enact age-of-consent laws,[17] and with *Samantha at Coney Island and a Thousand Other Islands* (1911), she continues educating her female readers on the most crucial social issues of her day, using humour as an indispensable rhetorical weapon.[18] By the time Holley wrote *Samantha on the Woman Question* (1913) and *Josiah Allen on the Woman Question* (1914),[19] she had replaced her pseudonym with her real authorial identity. As one biographer suggests, she did not want to hide behind "Josiah Allen's Wife" any longer, as she believed in the power of addressing a new generation of feminists directly.[20]

Jane Curry, who comprehensively studied how Marietta Holley used humour and satire to discuss and influence issues of gender equality, maintains that the nineteenth-century tradition of American humour fell into three categories: down east, southwest and literary comedians. The vernacular style was critical to all three categories:

> Vernacular or dialect humor was rendered in the language of the common person who eschewed the lofty syntax and vocabulary of standard English in favor of more familiar, down-to-earth idioms, generally conveyed through creative misspellings, extensive homey metaphors, and the insights of the wise innocent. These heroes and heroines were often uneducated, but were blessed with healthy doses of "horse sense" and "mother-wit." They applied their observations of life [...] to local, national, and even international topics.[21]

Inspired by literary comedians such as Artemus Ward and Bill Arp, Marietta Holley adopted the dialect of rural New York State,[22] devising proverbs and maxims spiced with homespun phrases.[23] Employing the tradition of

Yankee humour, which had already been established before the Civil War, Holley also added malapropisms, which the readers of her time found comedic.[24] Written in 1913, *Samantha on the Woman Question* focuses on women's rights and suffrage in particular.[25]

Krista Cowman, in her article "Doing Something Silly", contends that humour was a political tactic used by suffragettes in Britain during their campaign in 1903–14, and these suffragettes alleviated the stresses of the political campaign "by deliberately adopting 'silly' behaviours as a counterpoint to over-formal, male dominated [...] politics".[26] Unlike women novelists who deployed sentimental tropes to disseminate their progressive causes, Holley, as a prominent suffragist writer, used humour and satire as a novelistic strategy to critique social and political injustices, and, just as Cowman suggests, created female characters who adopt "silly" behaviours while asking for the right to vote.[27] This article analyses the propaganda value of *Samantha on the Woman Question* as a social novel which informs readers in a non-threatening way why female enfranchisement is necessary. It exonerates the American women's suffrage movement in the patriarchal public eye, while delicately refuting the anti-suffrage arguments of the president, senators and other prominent American social figures.

Holley's overall aim is to portray the plight of women across the nation, and how they are, in general, deprived of their social, legal, marital, political and economic rights. Holley does not portray Samantha as a suffering woman pursuing her own rights. Instead, she is an ambassador for her friend Serepta Pester, who "wanted the Whiskey Ring destroyed and her rights, and she wanted 'em both inside of two weeks" (4). Holley humorously narrates how women are deprived of their rights and bodily integrity as disenfranchised individuals: daughters are trapped in prostitution due to drunken fathers and brothers and the Whiskey Ring (5); widowed and unmarried women suffer from tax grievances due to man-made laws (5); mothers are left without children as fathers are granted custody and can easily give them away without the mother's consent (6); husbands acquire their wives' property on marriage due to the doctrine of coverture (8); "a woman can't testify in court, in any matter that is of mutual interest to husband and wife" (12); in the courts, women are tried and punished more severely than men "by the law [they have] no hand in making" (14); and men can beat their wives, and "the law of the United States don't approve of a man's whippin' his wife enough to endanger her life" (8). It is also implied that a man can legally beat his wife if she refuses sexual intercourse. Holley also criticizes Roosevelt's theory of race suicide by proclaiming: "Some men do git real wrought up about [race suicide] and want everybody to have all the children they can, jest as fast as they can, though wimmen don't all feel so" (10). She conveys through the use of satire that it has been

> [...] the boast of our American law that it takes care of wimmen. It took care of her. It held her in its strong protectin' grasp so tight that the only way she could slip out of it wuz to drop into the grave [...] Then it leggo. (7)

In the course of her criticism, Holley makes occasional references to important figures such as Susan B. Anthony and presidents Taft and Wilson, and to key suffrage events, including the 1894 New York State Suffrage Campaign, the great suffrage parade of 1913, and the militant activities of British suffragettes. She reveres and commemorates Susan B. Anthony, who died in 1906, observing her contributions to the movement and remembering how she became a target of sarcasm for male suffragists and anti-suffragists: "Susan's memory is beloved and revered, and the contemptuous ridicule of the onthinkin' and ignorant only nourished the laurels the world lays on her tomb" (45). Encounters with politicians are common in almost all the Samantha books. In fact, Samantha regards it as a personal duty to warn politicians about social and political inequalities, and to make recommendations accordingly.[28] In the novel, Samantha speaks to William Howard Taft, the twenty-seventh president of the United States and Wilson's predecessor, and decides that although Serepta "is justified [by the president] in askin' for her rights, and to have the [Liquor] Ring destroyed", Taft is "not the one to do them" (26). Holley then critiques his successor, President Wilson, and arrives at the same conclusion that "there are so many influences and hendrances planted like thorns in the cushion of that chair that a man, no matter how earnest he strives to do jestright, can't help bein' pricked by 'em and held back" (50).

The novel also makes occasional references to the 1894 New York Suffrage Campaign, when Susan B. Anthony planned "a house-to-house canvass to collect signatures on a mammoth woman suffrage petition".[29] Alluding to this campaign, Samantha humorously explains why the women in her town could not sign the petition, which reveals that these women prioritized their domestic chores over suffrage,[30] as they believed it was not worth their time. However, as Holley implies, such women ironically had the most to gain from political reform. Furthermore, Holley dramatizes the great suffrage parade of 1913, which occurred the day before Woodrow Wilson's inauguration, in an attempt to improve the image of the suffrage movement in American society. Despite the popular view that "a suffragist wuz a slatternly woman with uncombed locks, dangling shoe strings, and bloomers" (45), she observes that the suffragists in the parade were dressed decently in white and pink. She feels proud of the marchers and, through Samantha, Holley also praises the meticulous organization of suffrage activists and how their adeptness strengthens the movement. Through this suffrage parade, Holley also refutes the "cult of female frailty", an aspect of the nineteenth-century doctrine of True Womanhood, by stating:

> It wuz a burnin' hot day, and many who'd always argued that women hadn't strength enough to lift a paper ballot, had prophesied that woman wuz too delicately organized, too "fraguile" [...] to endure the strain of the long march in the torrid atmosphere. (58)

In a humorous way, she remarks that: "it wuz a surprise even to the marchers that of all the ambulances that kept alongside the Parade to pick up faint and swoonin' females, the only one occupied wuz by a man" (58). Holley also praises the efforts of the suffragists in a very patriotic way, underscoring the power of democracy. She persuades her readers to take a pro-suffrage stance because, unlike their militant British sisters:

> [...] our American Suffragettes employ the gentle, convincin' arts of beauty and reason. Some as the quiet golden sunshine draws out the flowers and fruit from the cold bosom of the earth. Mindin' their own business, antagonizin' and troublin' no one, they march along and show to every beholder jest how earnest they be. (57)

This event, for Samantha, is clearly more than a parade. In fact, she characterizes it as: "Good men and good women, each fillin' their different spears in life, but banded together for the overthrow of evil, the uplift of the race" (59). The speeches and arguments made by women suffragists from different states are so convincing that Samantha wonders "how anybody can help bein' converted to this righteous cause" (47). She believes that women's enfranchisement will uplift them to their righteous place, with "other good citizens of the United States"—in other words, side by side with (white) male citizens (she explicitly refers to race throughout the text) (47). Her spirit is contagious, and she even partially converts her complacent relative Lorinda and her anti-suffragist husband Josiah.

Holley also examines the militancy of British suffragettes through the Creation Searching Society, which was established by the leading men of Jonesville "for the purpose of searchin' out and criticizin' the affairs of the world, an' so far as possible advisin' and correctin' the meanderin's an' wrongdoin's of the universe" (3). The society convenes to discuss what can be done to help Englishmen who *suffer* at the hands of suffragettes, and what precautions can be taken to prevent the movement from spreading to America. Using humour, Holley conveys their ideas and, ironically, the action unanimously taken is proposed by an Englishman:

> [...] h'I propose if we can't do anything else that a card of sympathy be sent to hold Hengland from the Creation Searchin' Society of America, tellin' 'em 'ow our 'earts bleeds for the men's sufferin' and 'ardships in 'avin' to leave their hoccupations to beat and 'aul round and drive females to jails, and feed 'em with rubber hose through their noses to keep 'em from starvin' to death for what they call their principles. (188–89)

Here, Holley directly refers to the harsh treatment received by British suffragettes, including arrests and forced feeding. Even though she does not totally approve of their tactics, she empathizes with their militancy. However, she feels the need to differentiate between American and British suffrage campaigners. By saying that "there are no men so noble and generous as [...] American men" (57) and revering American manhood, she exonerates the movement in the public eye.

Feminism versus anti-suffragism in *Samantha on the Woman Question*

In *Samantha on the Woman Question*, Holley places Samantha on a mission to end women's legal inequality. She portrays her as an ardent feminist, but within limits. She is careful not to challenge, overtly at least, traditional gender roles or call into question Samantha's femininity, especially in terms of her domesticity. She defends feminist ideas through a feminized vernacular humour that relies on a "crackerbox philosopher's rural common sense".[31] Thus, she is able to avoid some of the more serious suffrage debates—such as that the vote would ruin American society by turning women into men —by bypassing them altogether. In the novel, Samantha's malapropisms are consequently more than just "being funny"—they are "an elucidation of social criticism" without the gravity of social criticism.[32]

For instance, Samantha uses the word "sect" instead of "sex", the women's "spear" rather than "sphere", and "Aunty" to mean the prefix "anti". As Curry maintains, by using the word "sect", Holley polarizes men and women, underscoring the fact that they are distinct groups. In this regard, using the word "sect" is a kind of othering. Likewise, by using the word "spear" for "sphere", she implies that the ideology of separate spheres can also be deployed as a weapon to bring about social change.[33] Holley also calls female anti-suffragists "She Aunties". By playing with the term "anti" and replacing it with "Aunty", she exposes the hypocrisy of wealthy anti-suffrage women with political power.[34] In the novel, Holley depicts Miss Vincent, who

> [...] wuz a ardent She Aunty and very prominent in the public meetin's the She Auntys have to try to compel the Suffragists not to have public meetin's. They talk a good deal in public how onwomanly and immodest it is for wimmen to talk in public. And she wuz one of the foremost ones in tryin' to git up a school to teach wimmen civics, to prove that they mustn't ever have anything to do with civics. (20)

Holley's description of the "She Aunties" could just as easily describe contemporary anti-feminist, patriarchal women, such as the Republican lawyer, politician and "housewife" Phyllis Schlafly, who rose to prominence during the Equal Rights Amendment battle of the 1970s and 1980s. Thus, Holley's characterization of such women is timeless.

Holley's use of homely wisdom and dialect was precisely designed to win over audiences harbouring anti-suffragist sentiments.[35] Receiving the same message from a young, liberated New Woman might have threatened the older generation of female readers. On the other hand, hearing the same message from an "uneducated", rural, "true" woman, with her "carefully crafted image of illiteracy and domesticity",[36] was entirely non-threatening. Throughout the novel, Samantha defends her cause on two fronts: she targets women who oppose women's rights and male politicians who are unwilling to take the necessary steps to enfranchise women. Her relative, Lorinda, who hosts the Allens in Washington, DC, is a foil character whom Holley devised to criticize Samantha's "unwomanly" ideals.[37] As Samantha narrates, having a rich husband and a comfortable life, Lorinda, like other middle-class anti-suffragist women, believes that women already have all the rights they need, and that voting would not solve, but would create, problems.

Holley also underscores how women are successful at municipal reform in those states where women could vote. Deriving strength from such prominent figures as Frances Willard,[38] Jane Addams,[39] and Theodore Roosevelt, she embraces "Home Protection"—the idea that American women need suffrage in order to preserve the home and motherhood. Taking refuge in this argument, Samantha tries to outwit Lorinda by asking:

> Do you think [...] if educated, motherly, thoughtful wimmen helped make the laws so many little children would be allowed to toil in factories and mines, their tender shoulders bearin' the burden of constant labour that wears out the iron muscles of men? (16)

Samantha believes that when women have equal legal power, they will be better wives and mothers because, with the help of the ballot, they will open schools to teach young girls how to keep healthy, comfortable homes and make themselves capable wives and mothers.

In *Samantha on the Woman Question*, Holley consistently refutes anti-suffragist sentiments during her encounters with senators. Senator A says: "Wimmen are the loveliest, most angelic creatures that ever walked the earth; they are prefect, flawless, like snow and roses" (28). He also maintains that "these angelic angels of our homes are too ethereal, too dainty to mingle with rude crowds" (29). His rhetoric exemplifies the patriarchal and paternalistic anti-suffrage arguments of the time, which posited that women should be in the home while men "took care" of business in the public sphere. This genteel tradition juvenilized women, deeming them sacred while undermining their existence, importance and intelligence. Not surprisingly, Samantha skewers the Senator by saying: "you call wimmen angels, and you don't give 'em the rights of the lowest beasts that crawl on the earth" (30). Despite sympathizing with the plight of women, the Senator compares the situation to slavery. Just like slave masters who could see the injustice of the "peculiar institution" but could not support change because the "old chains of Custom bound them", politicians, the Senator believes, are aware of the injustices suffered by women but cannot take action because their hands are tied by social customs (32).

Samantha also refutes the Senator's statement that: "the soft gentle brains of females are unfitted for the deep hard problems men have to grapple with. They are too doll-like, too angelically and sweetly frivolous" (33). This argument replicates those found in Molly Eliot Seawell's anti-suffragist essay "On the Absence of Creative Faculty in Women" (1891), which was ironically written by an intellectual woman.[40] Samantha, however, provides readers with examples of prominent women who contributed to humanity.[41] The Senator's claim that if these women were so important they would be represented in the Hall of Fame for Great Americans in New York City is refuted by Samantha, who argues that it would be so "if women formed half the committee of selection" (34)—clearly, a searing criticism of such a prominent American institution.

While it is difficult to assess the impact that *Samantha on the Woman Question* made on suffrage, the Samantha novels in general were certainly good propaganda for the cause. Both Frances Willard and Susan B. Anthony were so aware of the propaganda value of Holley's novels that they invited her to their conventions to give a speech.[42] When *Samantha on the Woman Question* was published in 1913, one-quarter of the states had already granted limited or full suffrage to women, and full enfranchisement for all American women came seven years later with the ratification of the Nineteenth Amendment. Appealing to the readers of her generation and the new generation of feminists, Holley refuted sentimental, pro-natalist arguments against women's rights, and tried to prove, through Samantha's cogent arguments, that women would not lose their virtue if they received the right to vote. Clearly, by refuting the irrational opposition of anti-suffragists with humour and satire, she, at a minimum, familiarized all readers, pro and con, with the cause of women's suffrage.

Women's suffrage, the settlement house movement and Elia Wilkinson Peattie

Journalism was another area through which women writers expressed their ideas. Elia Wilkinson Peattie used her journalism to disseminate her reforming zeal while entertaining readers with narratives comprised of fact, fiction or a blend of both. Born in 1862 in Kalamazoo, Michigan, to a ninth-generation American family, Elia Wilkinson Peattie was raised in Chicago, where she attended school until sixth grade. She married Robert Peattie, a reporter from the *Chicago Tribune*, in 1883, and took up writing with her husband, becoming the newspaper's first "girl reporter". The couple moved to Omaha, Nebraska, in 1888 and started working for the *Omaha World*

Herald, where Elia Peattie edited the women's page and wrote a weekly column.[43] Portraying new women like herself, who felt torn between the tenets of True Womanhood—piety, purity, submissiveness and domesticity—and the ideals of New Womanhood—emancipation, equality and opportunity—Peattie brought a fresh approach to journalism by writing factual editorials, crafting short, fictionalized narratives that supported her causes, and personalizing the news through fictionalized sketches based on real events.[44] Like her contemporaries, Peattie believed in the importance of collective action and became a grass-roots activist. Some of her achievements include the establishment of the Omaha Women's Club and later the Nebraska State Federation of Women's Clubs. As an ardent suffragist, she attended the national conference of the General Federation of Woman's Clubs in Philadelphia in 1894 to represent the Omaha Women's Club, sharing the stage with Susan B. Anthony.[45] In so doing, she gained prominence among suffragists and was more able to make contact with the female middle-class readership. Through club work, Peattie became an ardent advocate and spokesperson for women's rights. In the last decade of the nineteenth century, she travelled extensively around Nebraska to gather material for her writing on social injustice, municipal housekeeping, alcoholism, the annexation of Cuba, the Wounded Knee massacre, women's role in the church and unmarried mothers. Around the same time, Peattie returned to Chicago and started working as a literary critic for the *Chicago Tribune* between 1896 and 1917, becoming a prominent figure on Chicago's flourishing literary scene. She became a member of the book club Fortnightly and the Little Room Literary Club, and served as a leader in the Chicago Women's Club.[46]

Peattie authored numerous novels and short stories. As a mother of four children, she successfully balanced her domestic life with her career as an author. Elia Peattie was such a prolific writer that she published novels, plays, short stories and poems, as well as countless editorials, columns and book reviews until 1917. Her work was published in prestigious journals including the *Atlantic*, *Century* and *Harper's*. Many of her stories were collected in anthologies, such as *The Mountain Woman* (1896) and *The Shape of Fear and Other Ghostly Tales* (1898).[47] Her novels included *The Edge of Things* (1903); a series of children's books, *Azalea: The Story of a Girl in the Blue Ridge Mountains* (1912), *Annie Laurie and Azalea* (1913) and *Azalea's Silver Web* (1915); *The Precipice* (1914); and *The Angel with a Broom* (1915).[48] Elia Peattie died at the age of 73, in 1935, in Wallingford, Vermont.

Between the mid nineteenth and the mid twentieth centuries, middle-class American writers and reformers often "downclassed" in the name of reform, adopting a lower-class status in order to engage with those whom they sought to help. While male reformers regarded downclassing as part of investigative sociology, female downclassers, like Jane Addams, lived in settlements where they abandoned their creature comforts for the betterment of the underprivileged, and regarded the experience as self-renewing social work.[49] Elia Peattie's progressive novel *The Precipice* depicts the heroine's downclassing experience and her vital contact with impoverished mothers, fallen daughters and neglected children, much the same as Addams and other municipal reformers did.[50] However, embedded within this work is commentary about the abuses and inequalities faced by disenfranchised women.[51] Like its author, *The Precipice* embraces almost all the causes of the Progressive Era—especially women's suffrage—reiterating Peattie's convictions concerning municipal housekeeping. In the novel, the female protagonist, Kate Barrington, becomes a prominent social worker, who collaborates with Julia Lathrop and Jane Addams, both of whom recruit her to be the head of the Children's Protective League—a real organization established by Julia Lathrop. Kate devotes herself to her job, giving lectures throughout the country, and participates in events organized by the General Federation of Women's Clubs. Like many progressive women's social novels, *The Precipice* campaigns for a range of causes at the same time, from conservation to the elimination of vice, the plight of women workers to child abuse—in other words, numerous forms of municipal housekeeping within the settlement house movement, crowned by the cause of all causes: women's suffrage. In order to illustrate the urgency of women's enfranchisement, Peattie creates a progressive heroine, Kate Barrington, who prioritizes civic work over every other aspect of her life, including her love interest.

Although the suffrage movement seems peripheral in *The Precipice*, it in fact lies at the heart of the novel. At every turn, Peattie reminds readers of the necessity of enfranchisement, and underscores the fact that ordinary women's unhappiness and career women's restlessness are caused by disenfranchisement. In other words, through *The Precipice*, Peattie conveys that women in the city—educated or uneducated—suffer from the same inequalities and domestic burdens cast upon them as wives and mothers, which results from not being recognized legally and represented politically.

In *The Precipice*, Peattie regards urban society as an extended family, and provides her protagonist with an outlet—the corrupt city—in which to use her maternal powers.[52] Thus, in the novel, domestic abilities, which were formerly restricted to the private household, are transferred to the public sphere, with the metaphor of the family uniting both halves of society. In the same way that Holley makes reference to Susan B. Anthony, Peattie reveres and pays tribute to Jane Addams, who maintained that the city was "a great home" which accommodated a "civic family":

> [Jane Addams] was a woman with a genius for inclusiveness. She was the sister of all men. If a youth sinned, she asked herself if she could have played any part

> in the prevention of that sin had she had more awareness, more solicitude. It was she who had, more than others—though there was a great army of men and women of good will to sustain her—promulgated this idea of responsibility. (95)

Peattie describes social workers, such as Kate, who downclass as "the Addams breed', and suggests that she is a saviour who is "getting at the roots of our disease, and it's partly because she's a woman" (97).

Without downplaying women's roles as wives and mothers, Peattie relocates the concept of "biology as destiny" to the public sphere, where she integrates domesticity with a civic career.[53] Nevertheless, women like Kate still faced prejudice, malice and old-fashioned paternalistic rhetoric since, ultimately, they transgressed spheres and blurred social boundaries. Working with the impoverished, Kate becomes a more understanding and empathetic person, and her downclassing experiences have a healing effect on her soul. Social work brings meaning to her life:

> I used to feel like a person walking in a mist. But it's different now. Everything has taken on a clear reality to me. I'm even beginning to understand that I myself am a reality and that my thoughts as well as my acts are entities. (44)

As Peattie posits, being a social reformer strengthens a woman and enables her to view life from a different perspective. Moreover, her work helps her to heal not only herself but also others:

> If only women—all women—understood how to make true homes, there wouldn't be any need for people like us. We're only well-intentioned fools who go around putting plasters over the sores. We don't even reach down as far as the disease. (36)

Clearly, if women could get the vote, they would have more opportunity to reach the root of social problems since they would be participating in the law-making process.

As a New Woman, Kate believes that women need enfranchisement for spiritual reasons which anti-suffragists do not generally recognize. In the same vein as Holley in *Samantha on the Woman Question*, Peattie also mentions the common anti-suffrage arguments: that women should be kept as far away as possible from the dirty business of politics, and that anti-suffragist males are actually protecting women by not enfranchising them. However, Kate believes that

> [...] women desired the ballot because it was a symbol as well as because it was an instrument and an argument. If it was to benefit the working woman in the same way in which it benefited the working man, by making individuality a thing to be considered; if it was to give the woman taxpayer certain rights which would put her on a par with the man taxpayer, a thousand times more it was to benefit all women by removing them from the class of the unconsidered, the superfluous, and the negligible. (47)

At this point, Peattie uses the same argument as Holley, whose Samantha believed that enfranchisement would uplift women from the "unfit" class to that of the able-bodied, respected, decision-making citizen. Kate maintains that women's suffrage included potentiality, "and in potentiality is happiness" (47). As a social reformer, she is well aware that the arduous tasks which women perform to preserve the "great home" of America would be best served by the ballot. She believes that women were created with potential, and that they simply need opportunities to fulfil their potential. Just as liberty is regarded as an "ethic need of civilization" (48), enfranchisement, she deems, is necessary for women. Kate regards the ballot "as the best bulwark of liberty" (115), drawing attention to the fact that every woman requires it, regardless of education level or marital status, whether she is a rural housewife or an urban career woman. Although Kate is relatively independent, she still sees enfranchisement as an indispensable right, even for social reformers such as herself. Repeatedly, Peattie reminds her philanthropist readers (especially those in anti-suffragist women's clubs) of the necessity of enfranchisement, warning them that if they take a stand against women's suffrage, all the civic work they do to improve the lives of the underprivileged would ultimately be in vain:

> You toil for deserted children, indigent mothers, for hospitals and asylums, starting movements which, when perfected, are absorbed by the city. What happens then to these benevolent enterprises? They are placed in the hands of politicians and perfunctorily administered. Your disinterested services are lost sight of; the politicians smile at the manner in which you have toiled and they have reaped. You see sink into uselessness, institutions, which, in the compassionate hands of women, would be the promoters of good through the generations. (116)

In common with Holley's *Samantha on the Woman Question*, Peattie depicts a suffrage parade (which we assume to be the Chicago Suffrage Parade of 2 May 1914) in detail, glorifying the women who came together for a righteous cause: revolution. Yet she also portrays the backlash against the suffrage parade through the sexist male characters she creates. David, the husband of Kate's friend, finds the suffrage parade "uproariously funny" (81), and Ray McCrea, Kate's old friend, is surprised when he learns that Kate was "in that mess", and calls it "the Amazon march" (83). Although Ray appreciates her warring spirit, he laments that he feels ashamed "to find [Kate] marching with the militant women" (89). Again as in Holley's case, Peattie differentiates between the American and British suffrage movements. While sympathizing with British suffragettes, Peattie also strategically reveres American manhood. She does not approve of "acid-throwing and window-breaking" (184). As she states: "for one thing, it doesn't seem to me quite logical, as the damage is inflicted on the property of persons who have nothing to do with the case" (185).

The New Woman in *The Precipice*

In her column in the *Omaha World Herald* on 28 September 1895, Elia Peattie defines the New Woman:

> The woman who took herself inertly, who rested as she was made, neither watering her mind with knowledge nor cultivating her body by exercise, is no more to be compared to the cultivated woman than the wild plums to the perfect product of the carefully tended orchard.[54]

It is out of this definition that Peattie creates her heroine Kate Barrington, the ideal New Woman, who opposes women's identification with men at all costs. Thus, initially, she does not accept Karl's proposal. Rejecting the belief that a woman's place is with her husband, Kate criticizes the earlier generation of women, who acted "cowardly", fearing conventions:

> They had lacked the ability to utilize their powers of efficiency; had paid but feeble respect to their own ideals; had altogether measured themselves by too limited a standard. Failing wifely joy, they had too often regarded themselves as unsuccessful, and had apologized tacitly to the world for using their abilities in any direction save one. They had not permitted themselves that strong, clean, robust joy of developing their own powers for mere delight in the exercise of power. (47)

Throughout the novel, Kate is seeking independence: "I don't want to be protected. I mean I don't want to be made dependent; I don't want my interpretations of life at second-hand. I object to having life filter through anybody else to me" (146). Thus, she is looking for full partnership, without sacrificing intellectual compatibility, freedom or romance. As a New Woman, Kate wants to have it all, and demands "rights and privileges equal to those enjoyed by men" (189). Peattie allows Kate to proclaim her independence with her version of the "Declaration of Independence" on a precipice, during one of her mountain walks with Karl, the man she loves:

> I declare my freedom! [...] Freedom to think my own thoughts, preach my own creeds, do my own work, and make the sacrifices of my own choosing. I declare that I will have no master and no mistress, no slave and no neophyte, but that I will strive to preserve my own personality and to help all of my brothers and sisters, the world over, to preserve theirs. I declare that I will let no superstition or prejudice set limits to my good will, my influence, or my ambition! (190)

Peattie's use of the precipice for her declaration of independence is not coincidental.[55] Neither is the novel's title. Here, the precipice on which Kate stands as a strong New Woman metaphorically refers to the fact that being an independent woman is like standing on the edge. Although Karl implies that it may be fatal, Kate claims she will not fall, and if other women fall, this would be due to fear, "the most subtle of foes" (190).

Kate Barrington also influences the male protagonist she loves. Karl is a benevolent magnate of an industrial town who fosters self-respect among his employees, which does not exist in other industrial settings. By matching Kate and Karl—a municipal mother and a civic father—Peattie renders significant the "spousal trait of sharing elements of the settlement worker social philosophy".[56] However, as benevolent as he is, Karl bears traditional convictions, and Kate's ability to transform him comes into play at this point. The ending of the novel demonstrates how Karl, fearful of losing Kate forever, is converted:

> Go your way, Kate. Go to your great undertaking. Go as my wife. I stay with my task. It may carry me farther and bring me more honour than we yet know. I shall go to you when I can: you must come to me—when you will. What more exhilarating? (217)

Here, Peattie revises the traditional marriage plot.[57] While Kate is the New Woman, by the end of the novel, Karl Wander becomes the New Man. Their mutual partnership, as they rename marriage, sets an example for a new generation of feminists, and Kate remains "free and proud as the 'victory' of a sculptor's dream" (217). As Patrick Chura contends, Peattie is well aware that the complex needs of such a New Woman could only be met by a New Man. When he tells Kate that both can follow their own paths, Karl's public paternalism merges with Kate's public maternalism.[58] Thus, *The Precipice* serves as a vital catalyst for social change. Kate becomes a successful role model for personal and professional independence, showing women that they can balance career and home, as long as they are not afraid of standing on the precipice.

Conclusion

Although progressive women were influential in reform movements, their efforts were limited since they did not have the right to vote. Women novelists of the time informed middle-class audiences about the necessity of women's enfranchisement, even as anti-suffragist arguments remained fashionable. Marietta Holley was a suffragist novelist who, with *Samantha on the Woman Question*, adopted a literary trope unexpected of women writers at the time. Through satire, she allowed her protagonist, Samantha Allen, to use her horse sense, homespun wisdom and carefully woven sarcasm to persuade older women to abandon "moth-eaten" arguments about women's suffrage. By refuting anti-suffragist arguments using humour, she exonerated the movement in the public eye and, with her novels, became an influential figure in women's suffrage.

On the other hand, Elia Peattie encouraged women to seek careers, fight against vice and corruption, and, above all, acquire the vote. In *The Precipice*, the progressive protagonist, Kate Barrington, served as a successful role model for younger generations of women. Without transgressing her traditional role as a woman and potential mother, Kate deconstructs the "biology as destiny" argument and finds new meaning in her life through municipal housekeeping and balance. Conveying her beliefs through Kate, Peattie underscores the necessity of female enfranchisement, making women's suffrage a central issue.

Both novels approach women's suffrage from a mainstream, white, middle-class, Protestant, progressive stantce, the former by supporting uneducated rural women who are deprived of their rights, and the latter by promoting the modern woman, who personally and professionally proclaims her independence. All in all, both novels advocated suffrage and served as vehicles to enact social change. Without threatening socially accepted gender norms, both novelists and protagonists called on middle-class audiences to participate in the suffrage movement.

Notes

1. The plight of women who were working under hard conditions attracted the attention of reform-minded middle-class women, who especially wanted to improve the lives of poor, white Protestant women by changing society from within. To this end, progressive reformers worked under the roof of many benevolent organizations. They endorsed legislative goals, sending petitions to Congress to address specific social issues. Women's clubs allowed them to confront problems in a socially acceptable manner that worked within the confines of American gender roles—namely, by using their positions as daughters, wives and mothers to carry out projects to improve the lives of other daughters, wives and mothers. Invoking their maternal duties to protect children and care for the poor, the women of the Progressive Era created a civic awakening, known as "municipal housekeeping".
2. "Moral guardian" is the term used for the progressive women who tried to eradicate the social ills of society such as alcohol, prostitution and delinquency in order to improve the well-being of the home and the nation. Women of the Progressive Era acted as moral guardians, campaigning against all the forces that corrupt American society.
3. Marietta Holley, *Samantha on the Woman Question* (New York: Fleming H. Revell, 1913); Elia Wilkinson Peattie, *The Precipice: A Novel* (New York: Houghton Mifflin, 1914). Subsequent references are to these editions and given parenthetically in the text.
4. Founded in 1869 by Elizabeth Cady Stanton (1815–1902) and Susan B. Anthony (1820–1906), the National Woman Suffrage Association opposed the ratification of the Fifteenth Amendment, which enfranchised African American males. It focused primarily on a national amendment to grant women the right to vote, and openly discussed controversial topics such as contraception and divorce. The American Woman Suffrage Association, on the other hand, which was founded in 1869 by Lucy Stone (1818–93) and her husband Henry Browne Blackwell (1825–1909), supported the Fifteenth Amendment and focused on state-based constitutional amendments, avoiding the controversial issues that the National Woman Suffrage Association supported. Without doubt, such differences in approach marked a 20-year split in the women's suffrage movement, even delaying victory.

5. Ellen Carol DuBois and Lynn Dumenil, *Through Women's Eyes: An American History with Documents* (Boston: Bedford/St. Martin's, 2005), p. 425. Women in Washington, California, Arizona, Kansas and Oregon were enfranchised between 1910 and 1912 as a result of successful campaigns held at the state level, whereas the failures in Ohio, Wisconsin and Michigan encouraged suffragists to focus on a constitutional amendment.
6. Harriot Stanton Blatch (1856–1940) was the daughter of Elizabeth Cady Stanton. She received her education in England and came to the United States full of ideas of suffrage and equality. Initially working with the Women's Trade Union League, she founded the Equality League of Self-Supporting Women as the political wing of the Women's Trade Union League, which was later renamed the Women's Political Union, with the goal of bringing together elite women and working-class women under the umbrella of suffrage. See Ellen Carol DuBois, ed., *Woman Suffrage and Women's Rights* (New York: New York UP, 1998), p. 192. Blatch organized and led the 1910 New York suffrage parade, as well as militant street protests. Likewise, Alice Paul (1885–1977) and Lucy Burns (1879–1966) were also educated in England. When they returned to the United States, they joined the NAWSA, but were disturbed by its acquiescence under Anna Howard Shaw.
7. See Marjorie Spruill Wheeler, ed., *One Woman One Vote: Rediscovering the Woman Suffrage Movement* (Troutdale, OR: NewSage, 1995), p. 278.
8. Mary Chapman and Angela Mills, *Treacherous Texts: US Suffrage Literature, 1846–1946* (New Brunswick, NJ: Rutgers UP, 2011), p. 211.
9. Charlotte Templin, "Marietta Holley and Mark Twain: Cultural-Gender Politics and Literary Reputation", *American Studies*, 39.1 (1998): 75–91 (75). Templin suggests that in terms of style, Holley was likened to Mark Twain. Both Holley and Twain had the same publisher and the same illustrator, and were marketed in the same way, through subscription. Yet her male contemporary Mark Twain became one of the best-known literary figures in American history, while Marietta Holley remained in the shadows until she was rediscovered by 1970s feminists.
10. Marietta Holley, *My Opinions and Betsy Bobbet's* (Hartford, CT: American, 1873). The novel centres on the clash of ideas between a caricatured man-hunting spinster, Betsy Bobbet, and a practical rural woman, Samantha Allen (Josiah Allen's wife), who is a down-to-earth spokesperson for women's rights.
11. Holley, *My Opinions*, p. 12.
12. Margaret Wyman Langworthy, "Holley, Marietta", *Notable American Women, 1607–1950: A Biographical Dictionary*, ed. Edward T. James, Janet Wilson James, and Paul S. Boyer, vol. 1 (New York: Harvard UP, 1971), p. 203. In addition to the large sales, the popular success of the Samantha books was proven by the public readings, the successful dramatization by Neil Burgess, an American Vaudevillian comedian, and the demand from the publishers.
13. Marietta Holley, *The Lament of the Mormon Wife* (Hartford, CT: American, 1880); *Sweet Cicely: Josiah Allen as a Politician* (New York: Funk and Wagnalls, 1885).
14. Marietta Holley, *Samantha at Saratoga* (Philadelphia: Hubbard, 1887); *Samantha among the Brethren* (New York: Funk and Wagnalls, 1890).
15. Marietta Holley, *Samantha on the Race Problem* (New York: Dodd, Mead, 1892); *Samantha at the World's Fair* (New York: Funk and Wagnalls, 1893); *Samantha in Europe* (New York: Funk and Wagnalls, 1896); *Samantha at*

the St. Louis Exposition (New York: G. W. Dillingham, 1904); *Around the World with Josiah Allen's Wife* (New York: G. W. Dillingham, 1905).
16. Marietta Holley, *Samantha on Children's Rights* (New York: G. W. Dillingham, 1909).
17. Jane Curry, *Marietta Holley* (New York: Twayne, 1996), p. 76.
18. Marietta Holley, *Samantha at Coney Island and a Thousand Other Islands* (New York: Christian Herald, 1911).
19. Marietta Holley, *Josiah Allen on the Woman Question* (New York: Fleming H. Revell, 1914).
20. Kate H. Winter, *Marietta Holley: Life with Josiah Allen's Wife* (Syracuse, NY: Syracuse UP, 2005), p. 145.
21. Curry, p. xiv.
22. Nancy Walker and Zita Dresner, eds., *Redressing the Balance: American Women's Literary Humor from Colonial Times to the 1980s* (Jackson: UP of Mississippi, 1988), p. 98.
23. Lara Hernandez Corkrey, "Marietta Holley, Alice Duer Miller, the Rhetoric of Suffrage Humor, and the Changing Notions of Womanhood 1848–1920", PhD thesis, U of Kansas, 2007, p. 101.
24. Langworthy, p. 203.
25. The novel portrays a period in the life of Samantha and Josiah Allen, who decide to leave their fictional town of Jonesville to attend an Allen family reunion in Washington, DC. Samantha has other plans as well, such as conveying her friend Serepta Pester's concerns about women's legal rights to Washington politicians, and seeing the great suffrage parade that will take place the day before Woodrow Wilson's inauguration. However, Samantha is disappointed by her encounters with politicians, thus she directs her attention and enthusiasm to the suffrage parade, where she shares her opinions and observations with readers. Samantha's DC mission ends when they return home, where the local anti-suffrage group, the Creation Searching Society, gathers to discuss the militancy of British suffragettes and what they can do to stop it from spreading to America. Samantha overhears suggestions proposed by male members of the society (including her husband Josiah), which range from killing off the whole female race to poisoning them (reminiscent of Jonathan Swift's satirical 1729 work *A Modest Proposal*), to exiling them to a deserted location. The novel ends with Samantha outspokenly asking the male members of the society for the right to vote. Jane Curry claims that *Samantha on the Woman Question* is a reworked version of Holley's 1885 temperance novel, *Sweet Cicely*. Holley self-plagiarized complete sections from her earlier work and used them in her new novel. While Samantha's trip to Washington, DC and her encounters with politicians remained precisely the same, the suffering of female characters changed remarkably.
26. Krista Cowman, "Doing Something Silly: The Uses of Humour by the Women's Social and Political Union, 1903–1914", *International Review of Social History*, 52.S15 (2007): 259–74 (259).
27. Linda A. Morris, "American Satire: Beginnings through Mark Twain", *A Companion to Satire: Ancient and Modern*, ed. Ruben Quintero (Malden, MA: Blackwell, 2007), pp. 377–99 (391–92).
28. Winter, p. 4.
29. DuBois, p. 179.

30. For example, one of her neighbours, Ardelia, "couldn't sign it for lack of time". She was making a quilt, which took two years to finish, "so less important things had to be put aside" (3). Likewise, Ardelia's mother could not sign the petition because of the bedspread she was making, which took three years to complete: "She wuz quiltin' in Noah's Ark and all the animals on a turkey red quilt. I remember she wuz quiltin' the camel that day and couldn't be disturbed, so we didn't git the names" (3).
31. Carol Whitehouse, "Nineteenth-Century American Women Writers: Imagining Feminism", PhD thesis, Arizona State U, 2009, p. 4.
32. Curry, p. xviii.
33. Curry, p. xviii.
34. Curry, p. 78.
35. Corkrey, p. 103.
36. Corkrey, p. 103.
37. Curry, p. 78.
38. Frances Willard (1839–98), the founder of the Women's Christian Temperance Union, was a social reformer who also lobbied for women's suffrage.
39. Jane Addams (1860–1935) spearheaded the Settlement House Movement and created a civic awakening by founding the Hull House of Chicago. She improved the lives of many impoverished women and children, and was an active member of Theodore Roosevelt's Progressive Party.
40. Molly Eliot Seawell, "On the Absence of the Creative Faculty in Women", *The Critic*, 29 Nov. 1891: 292–294. Seawell (1860–1916) was a well-known southern regional writer of the time. In *The Ladies' Battle*, Seawell reflects her opposition to suffrage, saying: "I believe that the most important factors in the state are the wives and mothers who make of men good citizens to govern and protect the state, and I believe woman suffrage to be an unmixed evil". Molly Eliot Seawell, *The Ladies' Battle* (New York: Macmillan, 1911), p. 119.
41. At this point, Holley (Samantha) refers to the astronomer Maria Mitchell (1818–89), who discovered a comet with her telescope; the physicist Marie Curie (1867–1934), who pioneered research on radioactivity; the nurse Florence Nightingale (1820–1910), who "could mother and help cure an army" (33); and the novelist Harriet Beecher Stowe (1811–1916), whose story "thrilled the world and helped free a race" (34).
42. Langworthy, pp. 202–04. As contended by Langworthy, Holley was extremely shy, thus she never attended the conventions to which she was invited, yet she incorporated the material sent to her by Willard and Anthony into her novels.
43. Richard Walser, "Peattie, Elia (Maria Cahill) W.", *Dictionary of North Carolina Biography*, ed. William S. Powell, vol. 5 (Chapel Hill: U of North Carolina P, 1994), p. 54; Susanne George Bloomfield, *Impertinences: Selected Editorials of Elia W. Peattie, a Journalist in the Gilded Age* (Lincoln: U of Nebraska P, 2005), p. 5; Susanne K. George and Susanne George Bloomfield, *Kate M. Cleary: A Literary Biography with Selected Works* (Lincoln: U of Nebraska P, 2000), p. 15.
44. Bloomfield, p. 73.
45. Bloomfield, p. 13.
46. Bloomfield, pp. 12, 13, 163; Georgann Eubanks, *Literary Trails of the North Carolina Mountains: A Guidebook* (Hillsborough, NC: Copperline, 2009), p. 400; Walser, p. 54; Susanne K. George, "Peattie, Elia", *Encyclopedia of the*

Great Plains, ed. David J. Wishart (Lincoln: U of Nebraska P, 2004), p. 334; Rebecca Borden, "Conrad as a Provocation: Elia Peattie and the *Chicago Tribune*, 1903–1920", *Studia Neophilologica*, 85.1 (2013): 109–16 (109).

47. Elia Peattie, *The Mountain Woman* (New York: Doubleday and McClure, 1896); *The Shape of Fear and Other Ghostly Tales* (New York: Macmillan, 1898).
48. Elia Peattie, *The Edge of Things* (New York: Fleming H. Revell, 1903); *Azalea: The Story of a Girl in the Blue Ridge Mountains* (Chicago: Reilly and Critton, 1912); *Annie Laurie and Azalea* (Chicago: Reilly and Critton, 1913); *Azalea's Silver Web* (Chicago: Reilly and Critton, 1915); *The Angel with a Broom* (Chicago: Alderbrick, 1915).
49. Patrick Chura, *Vital Contact: Downclassing Journeys in American Literature from Melville to Richard Wright* (New York: Routledge, 2013), pp. 1–7.
50. The novel portrays the life of Kate Barrington, a graduate of the University of Chicago and the daughter of a tyrannical physician from Silvertree, Illinois. Disgusted with how her mother as a True Woman sacrificed her life, she leaves her father behind and moves to Chicago, experimenting with the possibilities the city could offer to a social reformer. Enmeshed within the novel's plot is a love story between Kate and her friend's cousin, Karl Wander. Karl is attracted to Kate, and during their conversations about love and marriage, they discuss the idea of a "mutual partnership" as a reworked version of companionate marriage. Karl proposes to Kate and asks her to stay with him in the mining town. Uninterested in sacrificing her independence for a man, she rejects his proposal. During a General Federation of Women's Clubs convention in southern California, Kate discovers she has been appointed head of the newly established Bureau of Children in Washington, DC, by the president of the Unites States (whom we assume to be Woodrow Wilson). During her absence from Karl, she contemplates her deep love for him. After the convention, she returns to the mining town to say farewell, but cannot suppress her feelings of love and longing. Finally able to reconcile her love with her independence, Kate finds a disappointed Karl on the precipice, or edge. They both propose a way to be happy without sacrificing the causes they deem important. They agree to maintain their relationship based on work, devotion, and equality. They decide to marry while pursuing their own agendas—Karl in his mining town and Kate in Washington, DC—with the hope they will reunite sometime in the future.
51. Jeffrey Andrew Weinstock, *Scare Tactics: Supernatural Fiction by American Women* (New York: Fordham UP, 2009), p. 70.
52. Sidney H. Bremer, introduction, *The Precipice*, by Elia W. Peattie (Champaign: U of Illinois P, 1989), pp. ix–xxvi (ix).
53. Timothy B. Spears, *Chicago Dreaming: Midwesterners and the City, 1871–1919* (Chicago: U of Chicago P, 2005), p. 193.
54. Elia Peattie, "A Word with Women", *Omaha World Herald*, 28 Sept. 1895: 8.
55. Borden, p. 109. Borden suggests that Peattie was inspired by the English novelist Joseph Conrad (1857–1924), who used the precipice as a metaphor for his heroine's limited choice between marriage and suicide in his novel *Chance* (1914), which was serialized in the United States between 1912 and 1913. In Peattie's novel, however, standing on the precipice epitomizes female freedom and determination, especially in terms of resisting Victorian notions of womanhood and embracing those of the New Woman.

56. Chura, p. 141.
57. Sarah Jo Lock, "The People in the Neighborhood: Samaritans and Saviors in Middle-Class Women's Social Settlement Writings, 1895–1914", PhD thesis, Texas Christian U, 2008, p. 184.
58. Chura, p. 141.

Disclosure statement

No potential conflict of interest was reported by the author.

ORCID

Emine Geçgil http://orcid.org/0000-0002-6521-7513

Index

Note: Page numbers followed by "n" denote endnotes.